The Psilocybin
MUSHROOM BIBLE

Virginia Haze and Dr. K. Mandrake, PhD

The Definitive Guide to Growing and Using
Magic Mushrooms

Green Candy Press

The Psilocybin Mushroom Bible:

The Definitive Guide to Growing and Using Magic Mushrooms

by Virginia Haze and Dr. K. Mandrake, PhD

Published by Green Candy Press

Toronto, Canada

www.greencandypress.com

ISBN: 978-1937866-28-0

Printed in China by 1010 Printing International Ltd.

Sometimes Massively Distributed by P.G.W.

Psychedelics are probably responsible for every aspect of human evolution apart from the decline in body hair.
— Terence McKenna (*Food of the Gods*)

CONTENTS

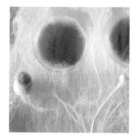

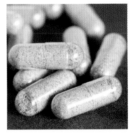

Dedication

It's not really us doing all this hard work. It's the cultures, and the grain, and the little mycelium growing from tiny spurts of nothing to huge underground creatures, forming webs of life underneath our feet. For us to take credit for this would be disingenuous; we're only thankful that we get to play around with such things, because it's huge fun.

Thanks to all those along the way who've taught us, and helped us, and listened to us talk and talk and talk some more. Thanks to the suppliers of much of our equipment, who we can't name, but without whose help this book would have probably never happened. A huge "gracias" also goes to Green Candy Press, without whom we'd still be chatting about a vague idea of a mushroom grow book but not getting anywhere with it.

Of course, thanks has to go to O. T. Oss and O. N. Oeric, otherwise known as Dennis and Terence McKenna, for starting off the psilocybin home grow revolution with their game-changing 1970s book *Psilocybin*. L. G. Nicholas and Kerry Ogame too contributed so much up-to-date cultivation knowledge with their more recent title *Psilocybin Mushroom Handbook*, and without these predecessors there's no way we'd even be growing our own shrooms, let alone writing a book about how to grow them. For this reason, we thank them wholeheartedly.

More contemporary research and frankly inspirational innovation is currently being undertaken by Paul Stamets, the American mycologist who holds a number of mushroom-related patents and who remains convinced that mushrooms can change the world for the better. If you've not yet watched Mr. Stamets's TED talk on *6 Ways Mushrooms Can Save the World*, we highly recommend it. Our copy of his book *Growing Gourmet and Medicinal Mushrooms* has been instrumental in taking us from hobby growers to serious cultivators and now to authors, and we would have been unable to write this, our own grow book, without the presence of his. If you want to further understand the world of mushrooms outside the sphere of psilocybin alone, you can buy no better book than his. Mr. Stamets: thank you, thank you, thank you.

As for online support, we would be lost without The Shroomery. There's a great community of growers, foragers and general mushroom enthusiasts who offer help and guidance at every step of the way. If you have any crazy ideas on how to modify our techniques, check if it's been tried in these forums (it probably has, and you can learn from others' mistakes / successes). One of the most prolific users, Roger Rabbit, is the arbiter of all things mycelial and has produced a great video for the *P. cubensis* grower called *Let's Grow Mushrooms*, which is definitely worth investing in. You can check out the whole thing at his website: mushroomvideos.com.

Disclaimer

In many countries across the world, the cultivation, manufacture, possession, use and supply of psilocybin is still bewilderingly illegal. These countries include the U.S., where psilocin and psilocybin are Schedule I drugs (though the sale of spores is legal in most states), the UK, where "fungi containing psilocybin" are Class A drugs, and Canada, where despite the sale of spore kits and grow kits being legal, psilocybin is illegal to possess, obtain or produce without a prescription or license.[1] [2] [3]

Schedule I drugs in the U.S. are those that are purported to have the following traits:

A. The drug or other substance has a high potential for abuse.

B. The drug or other substance has no currently accepted medical use in treatment in the United States.

C. There is a lack of accepted safety for use of the drug or other substance under medical supervision.[4]

Obviously we disagree with this, due to the massive amounts of evidence to the contrary, but the law is the law.

For these reasons, we recommend that all cultivation be done in Spain, where it's legal and where they serve a damn good local beer on a hot afternoon.

The authors of this book also don't recommend wearing Tyvek suits and cheap luchadores masks whilst performing lab work, cultivation work or in fact much at all; they're hot, flammable and you can't see a damn thing with the masks on as they cut right through your field of vision. However, if you need a semi-hilarious way to partially conceal your identity, they work pretty well.

Footnotes

1. Department of Justice, Drug Enforcement Agency of the United States of America. 2016. Online: http://www.deadiversion.usdoj.gov/schedules/orangebook/c_cs_alpha.pdf. Washington: Orange Book.

2. United Kingdom, Crime, Justice and the Law. 2016. Online: https://www.gov.uk/penalties-drug-possession-dealing. London: Courts, Sentencing and Tribunals.

3. Controlled Drugs and Substances Act of Canada. Online: http://laws-lois.justice.gc.ca/eng/acts/c-38.8/page-14.html. Ottawa: Justice Canada.

4. Controlled Substances Act, 84 Stat. 1236, 21 USC: Food and Drugs. See also: Wikipedia, 2016, Online: https://en.wikipedia.org/wiki/Controlled_Substances_Act#Schedule_I_drugs.

Introduction

You might have noticed, as you flicked through the first few pages of this book, that we decided to start out this comprehensive guide to psilocybin mushroom growing with a quote from Terence McKenna, the late American philosopher and psilocybin lover. McKenna was the Timothy Leary of the '90s; an incredibly influential figure who was as famous for his sometimes crackpot opinions (such as the belief that the Mayan calendar indicated that the world would end in 2012) as he was for his incredibly influential work on the relationship between humans and natural psychedelics.

So why start a book with a line from such a controversial figure? Well, in short, Terence McKenna did more for the mushroom home-growing revolution than almost anyone else. In 1976, McKenna and his brother, Dennis, published the first real guide to growing shrooms at home, entitled *Psilocybin: Magic Mushroom Grower's Guide*, using the names "O. T. Oss" and "O. N. Oeric." This book was the first to suggest to a widespread audience—an audience of flower kids and hippies, no less—that they could get high on their own supply, at home, for almost no money. By the time the new edition was published 10 years later, the book had sold over 100,000 copies, and it remains to this day one of the best mushroom grow guides

Your PF Tek cakes will be crowded with growing shrooms.

available, despite some attempts to better it.

However, that isn't all we have to thank Mr. McKenna for.

McKenna was the leading light in the world of psychedelics experimentation and study throughout his later life. He was one of the first to posit the theory that mushrooms might actually be alien to the Earth's ecosystem; that is, they might not have been here originally. He suggested that, because mushroom spores are subject to electrostatic forces, they could actually be carried out of the Earth's atmosphere or to the Earth from elsewhere—and because of their high survival rate and need for relatively little in the way of sustenance, they could easily colonize any worlds with decomposing organic matter on which they could feed. Of course, it would necessitate quite the cosmic accident for our world to have been subjected to mushroom spores in the first place—but the very possibility gives pause for thought at the least.

Regardless of the origin of psilocybin on Earth, McKenna's theory on the role that mushrooms might have played in human evolution is a fascinating one:

Whether the mushrooms came from outer space or not, the presence of psychedelic substances in the diet of early human beings created a number of changes in our evolutionary situation. When a person takes small amounts of psilocybin visual acuity improves. They can actually see slightly better, and this means that animals allowing psilocybin into their food chain would have increased hunting success, which means increased food supply, which means increased reproductive success, which is the name of the game in evolution.[5]

Paul Stamets also holds the view that mushrooms, both edible and psychedelic, have played an incalculable role in humanity's evolution. He opens his book *Growing Gourmet and Medicinal Mushrooms* with the words:

Humanity's use of mushrooms extends back to Paleolithic times. Few people—even anthropologists—comprehend how influential mushrooms have been in affecting the course of human evolution. They have played pivotal roles in ancient Greece, India, and Mesoamerica. True to their beguiling nature, fungi have always elicited deep emotional responses: from adulation to those who understand them to outright fear by those who do not.[6]

Your mushrooms MUST be properly dried to avoid mold.

Low doses of psilocybin improve visual acuity by increasing edge detection; you know when you indulge in just a couple of shrooms and the whole world starts to seem like it's in better focus? That's that exact thing at work. McKenna proposes that this actually would have helped primitive man to become more adept at catching food and therefore those who incorporated magic mushrooms into their diet, intentionally or otherwise, would have become more successful hunters; a necessary element for numerical propagation.

At slightly higher doses of psilocybin there is sexual arousal, erection, and everything that goes under the term arousal of the central nervous system. Again, a factor which would increase reproductive success is reinforced.[7]

This dedication to discovering the positive uses for psilocybin that go beyond just chewing on a few caps and getting ridiculously high is inspiring to us; it's what we strive to do, and we encourage you to as well. While there's absolutely nothing wrong with using psilocybin to relax, unwind your mind and have a good time, the potential for personal improvement is so huge that it seems a shame to ignore it. We certainly have tried to embrace this in our long association with psilocybin mushrooms, as both growers and consumers. We encourage you to do the same.

We've written this book with the intention of collating and more simply expressing the plethora of information that's available with regards to growing psychedelic mushrooms at home for personal use, as well as adding our own findings, techniques and recommendations. Whether you are a total rookie to mushroom growing, have carried out a number of successful non-psilocybin grows or have been growing for years and are looking to improve upon your set up, techniques and consumption options, we want this book to offer something to you. For years we've used the wonderful Paul Stamets book previously mentioned as our bible for edible mushroom growing, and we wanted to write something that would be just as useful for the magic mushroom grower.

It's like a maze in there! The gills of these shrooms are just fascinating.

Our approach to home growing is perhaps a little more scientific than some others, but we hope that we've been able to make our own methods approachable and understandable no matter what your level of skill thus far. You may only need the first few chapters in this book for a year or so, while you fine-tune the basis of mushroom growing and properly learn how to apply the methods herein. That's fine. You might discard the earlier part of this book and instead leap to the chapters about agar cloning or bulk substrate. That's fine also. But when you've amassed enough confidence to take your grow further, the latter chapters will be there to show you how to improve; or if you need a handy way to reference the basics even while you're completing a more difficult extraction method, the earlier chapters will be there to flick to and check what you

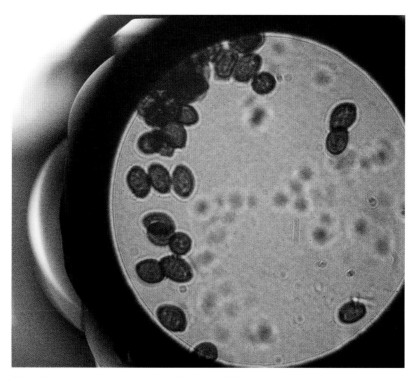

Under the microscope, you can see the intense life of the mushroom.

need. We hope, indeed, that there's something for everyone here.

We have assumed a very basic amount of prior knowledge in this book and in fact have aimed to explain every single step of the way as best we can. All you really need to start growing your own mushrooms is a willingness to learn and a little bit of resilience; we've all ruined batches and we continue to do so when we're being lazy and not following the techniques, but as long as you don't let any potential mistakes put you off for life, you'll soon be on your way to being a fantastic grower. If you are an absolute beginner, please don't let the heft of this book intimidate you; we don't bite! We were all once beginners and we approached our first grow with trepidation and a huge dose of anxiety. We're here to hold your hand through that first batch and help you to understand what, if anything, went wrong. Of course, being science folk and general hopeful overachievers, we've pushed ourselves to provide you with the best information that we can—so some of the content of this book will be beyond what you, personally, need to know. That's okay. You can skim over the bits you don't need. We won't be offended (much).

But why would you want to go further into the world of home mushroom cultivation anyway?

For one, it's a fascinating hobby. Mushrooms are almost infinitely interesting and the more you understand about them, the more gorgeously intriguing they become. There's quite literally more than meets the eye; while we usually just see the fruit of the mushroom, the bit that sticks arrogantly out of the soil, the real world of the mushroom begins beneath the ground, where mycelium can run for yards and sometimes even miles. It's impossible to consume mushrooms in the same way once you understand their frankly incredible life cycle. Being general hippie types and the sorts of people who'd rather spend four hours making a loaf bread than getting one from the supermarket down the road, we're firm believers in investing time and energy into producing things from scratch; if you're going to consume it, it's better to have a relationship with it. Understanding and appreciating the magic that goes into growing mushrooms has heightened our experience of tripping and given us a hell of a lot of respect for nature.

Being your own supplier obviously has a whole host of benefits in terms of health, purity, lack of adulterants, consistency, availability and cost, but

Second and third flushes often produce shrooms on the underside of PF Tek cakes.

Bigger is better. This shroom is somewhat misshapen, but it's still gorgeous.

pimping your grow can improve all of these two or even threefold. It can also mean that you spend a lot less time on dud grows and methods that don't work. We're hoping to show you methods that will be consistently successful and to teach you how to make the best of what cultures you already have. This will make your grow more secure as you'll spend less time sourcing spores from others and it'll save you money as well. With advanced sterilization methods you're less likely to get a mold infestation and ruin your grow space, and with better drying techniques you're going to avoid getting those disgusting rubbery shrooms that everyone forces down with a grimace. We'll also show you some advanced consumption methods that will allow for more accurate dosing and more delicious ways to get high, because everyone hates the taste of shroom tea even if they won't admit it.

Buying illegal substances from dealers is never ideal, as even the most trustworthy of sources can be a risk, and the quality of their product can never really be consistent. By making your own, you're quite literally taking this whole process in-house, and in doing so you are avoiding a lot of the risks of associating with a dealer. We should state here that we don't condone the selling of controlled substances. If you have any leftovers, give them away for free.

A word about security: if you're planning on engaging in growing where such an activity is illegal or frowned upon (and remember, we say you should do it in Spain), then it's worth considering how best to keep yourself safe and undetected. You should keep your grow set up as discreet as possible and preferably in a place where no one will stumble upon it in your house. Naturally warm areas of your house like near your boiler or in an airing cupboard are good choices for the early stages of growing, regardless of whether you need to be discreet or not. If you're short of space, it's easy enough to keep your stuff in the bottom of a wardrobe. However, once it comes to fruiting, your grow will need to be out in the open so it can receive some natural light. If your mum is coming over, hide the whole thing and lock it away; those mothers love to snoop.

In terms of procuring equipment and information, you might find that you have to buy a lot of your stuff on the web. While fairly non-incriminating things such as injection ports and jars can be bought from mainstream sites like Amazon without much bother, if you're buying industrial amounts of anything that might raise an eyebrow, it's best to invest in something that will keep you anonymous online. We use a VPN (Virtual

This shroom has literally bent over backwards to stay alive.

Private Network), and though we pay a small fee for ours, you can set up your own if you have the requisite know-how. However, we don't, so we pay a little and we can rest safe in the knowledge that our IP addresses are always hidden and no one can track us. TOR can also be a great help when hoping to stay anonymous online.

Always have any purchases sent to an address that's not the same as the address at which you're growing. If you're buying spores on the web, ensure that the company that sends them will do so in discreet packaging and preferably within your country; when things like syringes are sent internationally, that's when things start to get messy and potentially dangerous. The best option is always to buy things in person, with cold hard cash, but that's most likely not possible for everything you will need. Ensure

These mushrooms should have been picked a few days ago.

that you're not leaving a paper trail that leads straight from a mushroom growing website to your house. The methods that we'll show you in this book will allow you to make a consistent source of spores from just one spore syringe, meaning you should no longer need to buy spores from any other sources.

In this book we'll also show you how to make a stir plate and how to sterilize using a pressure cooker. When undertaking anything like this, put your best Safety Steve hat on and don't take any chances. If you're not great with wiring, watch some YouTube videos, educate yourself until you're confident and make sure you follow instructions to the letter. If you haven't used a pressure cooker before and yours looks a bit dodgy, read the instructions then call your mum. She'll be pleased that you're finally eating better and she'll be keen to help. Don't handle or move incredibly hot things and don't leave things in the cooker longer than they need to be. When glass is hot, use oven gloves. When things are sharp, be careful. Dispose of old needles in a sharps box if you have one, but if not, place the cap back on, tape it closed, wrap it in cardboard and get rid of it safely. Basically, treat needles as if they were bits of broken glass. And if anything

The slats in a sushi-rolling mat allow for great airflow to your drying shrooms.

ever gets moldy, throw out everything affected, sterilize all your equipment and never, ever put non-food-safe items where food might be. Wear gloves, and if you're not wearing gloves, wash your hands.

When it comes time to dispose of your leftover growing bits and bobs, move them out of your growing space at night and as inconspicuously as possible. While it might seem a good idea to throw everything in a bin bag, that can actually look suspicious as hell, so stacking things in cardboard moving boxes and lifting them into the trunk of your car might be better. Get rid of your organic materials at an off-site composting area, and make sure that anything you get rid of cannot be traced back to you. Try not to lug things like a glove box around in broad daylight unless you've got a plausible excuse (maybe you're a science student, or maybe you have another hobby that might explain you having such a thing).

Most of all, don't accidentally become the guy that everyone comes to for their shrooms. While it's natural to want to show off your killer growing skills to everyone who will listen, the best advice is this: shut up. The fewer people who know about what you're doing, the fewer people there are to accidentally rat you out or tell some strangers where they're getting their stash from. Loose lips sink ships, or something like that, and while your friend Daryl might be fun to trip with, he might also be absolutely terrible at keeping secrets, so keep him in the dark. If you have some extra, pass them on to trusted friends. Never let the word get out that you're selling, or you'll find that you're inundated with phone calls on a Friday night when everyone's drunk and wants to get high, and it only takes one idiot with a loud voice to shout up to your apartment from street level before the whole block is calling you That Guy With All The Shrooms. There's no middle ground between Drug Dealer and Not Drug Dealer, so be careful taking that first step.

This guy has grown up the side of a monotub. Good on you, buddy!

While we hope that readers all over the world will benefit from reading this book, we can't offer specific information for the dates and length of time of the potential growing season for every place in the world; the variables for growing are just too different in Sydney than they are in Alaska.

It's fascinating to watch your mushrooms grow, especially when they're small.

However, there's a great rule of thumb for when your mushroom-growing season should start and finish: if you're comfortable enough to walk around your house naked, then you can grow.

We should add that we mean comfortable in terms of temperature here; whether or not you're happy to get your kit off in social situations has no bearing on when you should start your grow op.

In places like New York, Chicago and Toronto, this might mean that you start growing in April, and in California this might be even earlier. This isn't likely to be exactly the same as the optimum growing months in your location. Where we live, it's always depressingly cold even into April and May, so we often wait until the end of May to get our grow going and we stop around September or, if we're very lucky, October. Growing any later than that would be a waste of time and energy. Plan your growing season accordingly and optimize the time you do have by planning ahead.

A final word: this is a guide. None of the information in this book is prescriptive. We've given you figures that have worked for us and offered potential additives and changes to these figures where applicable. Hopefully what we've done inspires you to play around with the recipes and methods, to understand what's happening in your mushroom grow, and

As the veil tears away, it becomes papery and almost ethereal.

to learn further yourself. Don't feel the need to follow our advice to the letter every time. The mushrooms will grow. They are biologically evolved to do so. All you need to do is provide conditions that are more favorable for the type of growth that you desire to give you the amount of mushrooms that you desire. All the rest is nature.

How to Use This Book

We've written this mushroom cultivation guide with the goal of providing a one-stop resource for mushroom growers. We've aimed to show every step of the process via step-by-step illustrative photos and explicitly clear text instructions for mushroom cultivation indoors. We know how difficult it can be to properly pull off a new growing method or your first crop when you're worrying about sterility and safety as well as getting it right, so we've attempted to make this as simple as possible.

In Chapters 1 and 2 we'll give you an overview of mushrooms in the *Psilocybe* genus and tell you where and how to safely source spores. In Chapters 3, 4 and 5 we'll teach you about good practice and sterile technique, allowing you to maintain a clean, successful workspace and avoid contamination, and then we'll go over what equipment and supplies you'll need as well as showing you how to make your own hardware for growing. These first five chapters are to prep you for mushroom cultivation and to ensure that you have everything you need before you start.

Chapters 6 to 10 outline the five main grow methods that we use, increasing in difficulty as the book progresses. These methods feed into and complement each other, and a good, progressive growing operation will ideally use all five. However, we've also written these in the order in which they should be taken up—at least in our minds. For instance, Chapter 6 outlines PF Tek, which is traditionally the technique that indoor growers first use. You could stop here if you really wanted to, simply doing the basic PF Tek method (or our variation on it) over and over again. However, if you want to go further, you can then learn how to create your own liquid culture in Chapter 7, in order to have a consistent source for spores. If you then wish to scale up your grow and diversify your substrate, Chapter 8 discusses cultivation on grain. This then feeds into Chapter 9, Bulk Substrate Method and Pasteurization, which will allow you to scale up your growing operation even further and get huge yields for next to no effort. Chapter 10 introduces agar work, which will allow you to maintain and purify culture lines, clone from tissue, isolate strains and safely store your culture.

A great grower will learn to utilize all these techniques in conjunction with each one, using one or another where it is most appropriate. For instance, new growers, those with less space in which to grow or those who don't need huge amounts of mushrooms will turn to PF Tek, as this is a fantastically simple method that can be done once in a while, to top up your shroom stash whenever you need it. Such a grower might delve into liquid cultures to ensure that they have a good source of spores for their thrice-yearly crop. Another grower, however, might be looking to assemble a consistent growing set up and so will turn to grain work, in order to inoculate bulk substrates and therefore yield huge amounts. This second grower may find that a combination of liquid culture, grain and bulk substrate work is perfect for them. Yet another grower may be keen to delve into the more scientific side of growing, in order to work with cleaner cultures and experiment with cloning. Such a grower will want to delve into agar work in conjunction with whatever method they're choosing for their main grow. This book allows you to tailor your growing style to your own needs.

These PF Tek jars are all colonized and ready to be "birthed."

After we've covered all the methods mentioned, we'll move on to troubleshooting and understanding contaminants in Chapter 11. After that, it's down to the serious business of post-harvest activities; Chapter 12 covers making more sprints and syringes, drying your mushrooms and properly dosing once they're good and ready. In Chapter 13 we show you many ways to consume your shrooms, and in Chapter 14 we briefly discuss the research into psilocybin as medicine. Resources, glossary and an index follow, as you can never have too much information.

In short, this book aims to give you all the information you need and aims to teach you enough so that you can decide exactly what methods to use and when. We want you to be a smart and independent grower. We know you will be.

Shall we begin?

Footnotes

5. Terence McKenna, interviewed by David Jay Brown and Rebecca McClen. *High Times* magazine, April 1992. See online: http://deoxy.org/t_highx.htm.

6. Paul Stamets. *Growing Gourmet and Medicinal Mushrooms*, 3rd Ed. 2000. San Francisco: Ten Speed Press, at 1 [Stamets, *Gourmet*].

7. Supra note 5 [McKenna].

Chapter 1

Mushroom Basics

The Different Parts of a Mushroom

Mushrooms are like icebergs; there's a hell of a lot going on under the surface. In fact, the part of the mushroom that you see sticking out of its growing medium is only half—or less—of the picture.

The top part of the mushroom, the part we see all the time, is called the fruit, or sporophore. This fruit consists of a stalk and a cap. The stalk is able to absorb water, while the cap's main function is to unfold when the fruit reaches near-maturity and then drop spores, from which new mushrooms can be created. The bottom part of the mushroom, the part underneath the soil, is called the mycelium. The mycelium is really the mushroom itself, while the top part is simply the expression of the fruit. The mycelium's job is to gather food for the mushroom. While the fruit of the mushroom only lives for a matter of weeks or even days, the mycelium are relatively invincible; with enough food and a large enough growing medium, they can actually live for hundreds of years. The fascinating relationship between these two parts of the same organism was put beautifully by Paul Stamets:

The mycelium is a fabric of interconnected, interwoven strands of cells.

The caps of the same species can be different shades and shapes.

P. cubensis *caps turn from orange-brown to golden brown as they mature.*

One colony can range in size from a half-dollar to many acres. A cubic inch of soil can host up to a mile of mycelium. This organism can be physically separated, and yet behave as one.[8]

Mycelium are so fascinating that entire books have been written about them. Mr. Stamets's sixth book, *Mycelium Running: How Mushrooms Can Help Save the World* is a must-have for anyone who wants to understand how these things work. Mycelium consist of threadlike hyphae that grow downwards into the cultivation medium then spread and spread and spread in search of food and sustenance for the mushroom. They achieve this by secreting enzymes onto the complex food source, breaking it down, then absorbing the resulting monomers (simple sugars, amino acids and minerals). This is called extracellular digestion.

This food is then sent to fortify the fruit of the mushroom, which emerges from the mycelium and into the air, first as a little pinhead of an organism and then grows upwards into the mushroom shape that we know. Caps emerge from the growing stalks, and eventually these caps open up to reveal the gills underneath and the spores that fall from there. A veil protects these gills until the mushroom is ready to drop the spores; at that point, the veil will break, leaving some on the stalk as a reminder of where it was attached. When the spores have been dropped, the fruit will stop trying to sustain itself. It's for this reason that we, as home growers, should harvest our fruit just before the spores are dropped. But we'll get to that later; first, let's have a look at the life cycle of a mushroom in more depth.

The mycelium is the network of interwoven cell strands that really constitutes the mushroom.

Mycelium spreads and becomes more threadlike as it feeds on the substrate.

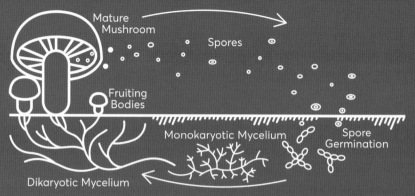

Mature Mushroom

Spores

Fruiting Bodies

Monokaryotic Mycelium

Spore Germination

Dikaryotic Mycelium

The Life Cycle of a Mushroom

Technically, the life cycle of a mushroom begins when the parent mushroom (the mushmom, if you will) drops spores from its gills. These spores are more accurately called haploid basidiospores, meaning that each one contains half

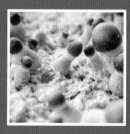

The "fruit" of the mushroom first emerges as a pinhead of an organism.

the genetic material needed for a mature, actively fruiting mycelium. Put simply, they quickly germinate into monokaryotic mycelium, which cannot sexually reproduce on their own. These monokaryotic mycelium will grow until they encounter the monokaryotic mycelium of the same species. These will then join together through "clamp connections" and share their nuclei to form a single dikaryotic mycelium, which is then capable of producing mushrooms. This dikaryotic mycelium is a quicker growing, more vigorous type, which quickly creates a web of underground threads. An environmental change, such as the intro-

duction of light, a drop in humidity or a reduction in CO_2, all of which are experienced when mycelium nears the soil surface, is a signal for the mycelium to begin fruiting. The first small bodies of the fruit pop upwards out of the growing medium to create fruiting bodies; in layperson's terms, a mushroom.

The stem of this fruit will grow over a matter of days, and as it grows, the cap will begin to unroll itself and unsheathe its gills, which will drop spores as the fruit reaches final maturity. Thus, the process begins all over again.

P. cubensis will grow on a number of materials, including a brown rice substrate.

Why Do They Get You High?

Not all mushrooms get you high—which is good, otherwise having a fungi risotto with your Italian grandma would get real weird real quick. However, there are over 200 species of mushroom that do contain psilocybin, the naturally occurring chemical compound that makes you trip.

When we ingest psilocybin-containing materials, the body quickly gets to work metabolizing that psilocybin to psilocin, which is able to bind to our serotonin receptors (more accurately put, psilocin is a partial agonist for our serotonin receptors). Psilocin is the compound that causes the primary effects of a mushroom trip. Psilocybin is considered a pro-drug: a compound that is inactive but is metabolized into a pharmacologically active compound in the body, in this case psilocin. Serotonin is structurally similar to psilocin, but it is actually a monoamine neurotransmitter, and it's the source of all those happy, fluffy feelings of well-being that you get from both general life and from chemical assistance. As a neurotransmitter it also helps to relay messages

These little mushrooms will grow so quickly you can almost watch them.

This Is Your Brain on Drugs

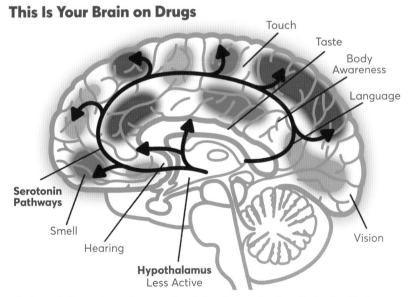

Touch

Taste

Body Awareness

Language

Serotonin Pathways

Smell

Hearing

Vision

Hypothalamus
Less Active

The hypothalmus shows decreased activity when under the effects of psilocin.

These purple spores have been dropped by a mature mushroom inside a terrarium.

This PF Tek mushroom still has some of the medium on its stem.

from one part of the brain to another. Research currently suggests that the sensory overload that forms a trip occurs because psilocybin causes the brain to become hyperconnected; that is, it allows for greater communication between parts of the brain that don't usually "talk" to each other so much. It is said to reorganize connections and strengthen weak ones, creating phenomena such as synesthesia.

Your brain has evolved to constantly filter out any non-useful stimulus, enabling you to focus on the important task of being a human being. As a result it saves its resources without getting bogged down in trivialities such as how many cars you saw on the street today, or why the light hits the trees in such a beautiful way in the park.

Regions of the brain thought to be responsible for inhibiting distracting stimuli and helping maintain attention, such as the hypothalamus, have shown decreased activity when under the effects of psilocin. These regions are usually some of the most active in the brain and play important roles both in organizing incoming sensory information and regulating internal impulses according to socially acceptable behavior.

This idea of the brain as a control center, which filters external stimuli and controls subconscious impulses, is echoed in literature. Aldous Huxley describes the "Mind at Large" as the overwhelming set of sensory information that is ultimately whittled down by the brain to that which is most important:

> Each person is at each moment capable of remembering all that has ever happened to him and of perceiving everything that is happening everywhere in the universe. The function of the brain and nervous system is to protect us from being overwhelmed and confused by this mass of largely useless and irrelevant knowledge, by shutting out most of what we should otherwise perceive or remember at any moment, and leaving only that very small and special selection which is likely to be practically useful. According to such a theory, each one of us is potentially Mind at Large.[9]

When the compound wears off, these connections go back to "normal" and we go back to feeling somewhat dulled but much more stable. Or boring, if you will.[10]

Psilocybin is pharmacologically similar to lysergic acid diethylamide, better known as LSD, and to phenethylamine-containing alkaloids like mescaline. This helps to explain why many of the effects of the drugs overlap; specifically, altered sense of colors and sounds, altered sense of self, visual and audio hallucinations and time and space dilation.

Serotonin

Psilocybin

Psilocin

Lysergic Acid Diethylamide (LSD)

Mescaline

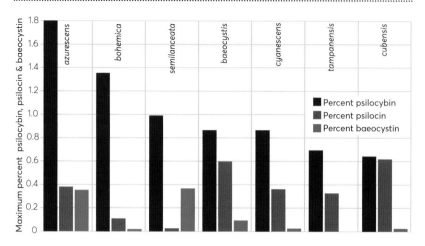

A comparison of maximum reported percentages (dry weight) of psilocybin, psilocin and baeocystin in 12 species of **Psilocybe.** *Source: Paul Stamets.* Psilocybin Mushrooms of the World: An Identification Guide, 1996. San Francisco: Ten Speed Press.

Different Species of Psilocybin Mushrooms

The most potent types of psilocybin-containing mushrooms are those from the genus *Psilocybe*. Mushrooms of this genus are usually pretty small, but they can be found all over the world. We'll briefly discuss some of the more common or interesting species, then explore a little more about our chosen species as well as explain why we've chosen it. We won't go too in depth here, as much has been written about the different types of mushrooms and we don't want to bore you to death, but if you are interested in learning a lot more about the intricacies of these species, we recommend *Psilocybin Mushrooms of the World: An Identification Guide* by Paul Stamets (1996).

Psilocybe semilanceata a.k.a Liberty Caps

Liberty caps have the double honor of being one of the most common species of *Psilocybe* and also one of the most potent. As well as containing psilocybin, liberty caps also contain the psychotropic tryptamine baeocystin, which is an analog of psilocybin and is said to be just as psychoactive, though it is relatively underexplored. In presentation, these mushrooms are quite distinctive, in that they have long, thin stipes (stalks) and yellow or brown bell-shaped caps that grow to around 1 inch in diameter and are topped with a point that looks not unlike a human nipple. As the spores mature they turn purple-brown rather than the blue-green of some other species.

Liberty caps are a favorite of some and they can be found growing in the wild in the more temperate regions of the Northern Hemisphere, as well as some places in South America and Australia. They grow in fields and meadows and particularly love wet soil that's been fertilized with livestock dung. However, this species feeds off decaying grass roots rather than animal feces. Liberty caps are relatively difficult to grow and even to find spores for, depending on where you are in the world, although more dedicated home growers do cultivate them indoors and treasure them as much for their challenging growing manner as for their intense effects.

Most psilocybin mushrooms "bruise" blue when handled, as you can see here.

Growing between other shrooms has left this mushroom looking like Beyoncé at a wind machine.

Psilocybe cyanescens a.k.a. Wavy Caps

This is another particularly potent species, though wavy caps contain only psilocybin and psilocin in significant amounts. These mushrooms can be identified by their flat, caramel-colored caps that become slightly wavy when the fruit reaches maturity, hence their nickname. These caps can reach up to 2 inches in diameter and sit atop a tall, medium-thin stipe. Wavy caps don't have a pronounced veil over their gills like other species, and the spore print is dark brown to purple.

This species grows primarily on wood chips but doesn't like bark as a substrate, and it can be found all along the West Coast of the States as well as Central and Western Europe, Australasia and Asia. Wavy caps can sometimes grow in absolutely enormous quantities in the wild, so if you do stumble on one of these massive patches, you're in luck! It can be difficult to grow this species in an indoor environment, as fruiting is brought on by a drop in temperature rather than an exposure to light, meaning that you have to bring the temperature in your grow area down to around 50°F (10°C), place the colonized jars in the fridge (and remove them twice daily to receive some light) or strategically grow at the end of summer. Either way, it's not easily done and is time-consuming at best.

Psilocybe azurescens a.k.a. Azies

Azies, as they're affectionately known, are perhaps the strongest mushroom in the genus *Psilocybe*. They contain up to 1.8% psilocybin, 0.5% psilocin and 0.4% baeocystin by dry weight, making them a hell of a fun experience for anyone who gets their hands on them. These shrooms are small, with a cap measuring half an inch or less and a stipe that only grows to three-quarters of an inch above ground. The cap fades from brown to caramel and then to beige, and the spore print is dark purple to black.

This species grows well on wood chips and in soils that are heavy in sand, and for that reason it can be found not too far away from the coast, often growing in tight clusters. However, azies have almost never been successfully cultivated indoors. While growers have inoculated them into rye berries, which are then spawned onto wood chips, most have then moved the grow to an outdoor substrate. To grow this species indoors would require phenomenal environmental control as well as very low temperatures and large amounts of light. A modified refrigerator would work

The caps of these mushrooms have been stained by the spores of their taller compadres!

in theory, but putting this into practice is another matter altogether. Still, there's nothing to say that you can't be the pioneer we need in this field! Reach for the stars!

Psilocybe tampanensis

It's incredibly unlikely that you'll come across this species of *Psilocybe*, either in the wild or in someone's grow room. *P. tampanesis* is incredibly rare; it was discovered in Florida and then found in Mississippi at a later date, but it is not often seen. Thankfully, someone had the foresight to clone that first Floridian sample, and the offspring of this clone have been in circulation ever since, though it is still relatively unlikely you'll see them unless you go looking for them. This species grows tall on a thin stipe, with yellow-brown convex caps that flare out at the bottom, but it also produces truffle-like sclerotia (a hardened mass of mycelium), better known as philosopher's

12

stones, which are consumed for psychedelic purposes just like the fruits themselves. We've had them, and they do the job. Interestingly enough, these sclerotia actually protect the fruits from wildfires and other disasters.

Psilocybe mexicana

This is a relatively common and somewhat unassuming species, albeit one with a long and important history. Besides being known and loved by the Aztecs as well as a number of other native communities throughout Central and North America over 2000 years ago, it was *P. mexicana* that arguably kick-started our appreciation for and understanding of the magic mushroom in the modern age. Dr. Albert Hofmann, the godfather of the LSD revolution, worked extensively with this species and was the first to isolate and name the psilocybin and psilocin compounds. So we've got a lot to thank *P. mexicana* for.

The fruits of this species have a distinctive striped, conical cap that's beige with light brown lines, atop a long, thin, darker brown stipe that grows between 2 and 4 inches in height. The spore print is dark purple to brown, and the fruits can also grow sclerotia, or philosopher's stones, like *P. tampanensis*.

P. mexicana grows on moss and mossy soil, most commonly along roadsides and more humid areas. The fruits grow in small groups, and the species can be most commonly found in Mexico, Costa Rica and Guatemala.

Psilocybe baeocystis
a.k.a. Bottle Caps or Bluebells

This is the species that really puts the "bae" in *baeocystis* (sorry). It's not the species that contains the largest percentage of baeocystin, but rather the species in which the compound was first found. The fruits of this species consist of a tall stipe, about 3 inches long and brownish white in color, with a dark olive-brown cap that turns inwards towards the stipe. Both the stipe and the cap will bruise easily and turn blue; sometimes the fruit can appear entirely as a metallic-blue color, and when they do they look incredible. The spore print is purple to brown and the gills are caramel colored.

P. baeocystis is most commonly found on bark, wood chips, peat moss, mulch and sometimes on lawns and in grassy areas, though this is rare. They can be found sometimes growing underneath other plants in gardens, and when bruised blue all over are very obvious to spot.

They look almost angelic, don't they?

Here the veil has started to pull away so this mushroom can drop its spores.

Here you can see the gills of the mushroom, which drop the spores.

These babies have sprung from the mycelial growth on a horse-manure substrate.

Psilocybe cubensis
a.k.a Golden Tops, Cubes, Gold Caps

If you've heard of any of these species already, it's most likely this one. *P. cubensis* is the most common type of *Psilocybe* grown indoors, and it's the one we'll be growing throughout this book. The reasons are manifold. First of all, and most importantly, they're both easy to grow and forgiving to new growers; you can make mistakes with cubes (as they're affectionately known) and they can take it, to an extent. Not only do they grow happily on a variety of different substrates, they also pin easily, and a small *P. cubensis* grow can be scaled up to a larger grow without too much additional effort.

They're also as easy to locate as they are to cultivate and are found all the way across North America, Asia and South American countries like Peru and Ecuador, though the species was first documented in 1906 in Cuba, the place from where it got its name. This species is coprophilous meaning that it grows best on the dung of herbivores like cows and horses, though as we'll show in this book it will happily colonize substrates made of brown rice flour, popcorn, birdseed and several types of grain. It prefers a humid

This is some fantastic and vigorous rhizomorphic growth!

Tomentose growth around the base of some shrooms. This is not mold!

environment, which is why it grows particularly well in subtropical climates, especially in river valleys. However, its ease of home cultivation is what makes it a favorite amongst growers; Terence and Dennis McKenna made *P. cubensis* famous when they described it as the easiest psilocybin mushroom to grow at home.

Cubes have a broadly convex cap and turn from orange-brown in their youth to golden brown as they mature. They can grow up to 6 inches in height, although around 4 inches is more common. The spores are purple to brown. Cubes contain psilocybin, psilocin, baeocystin and norbaeocystin, making them relatively potent but not crazily so.

The traits of *P. cubensis* really do make it the perfect strain to grow at home. Your crop won't be unmanageably large, and the way the fruits grow makes them easy to deal with and easy to understand. They tolerate a range of humidity levels and can cope with being handled to an extent. We're making an assumption in this book that the goal of most home growers is to put together a consistently successful grow operation that brings in a good harvest of moderately strong mushrooms with the strongest return

Rhizomorphic growth appears as the stringy, thready bits you can see here.

The stem of this fruit goes from white to beige with streaks of brown.

on investment possible; that is, the best trip for the least money and effort. *P. cubensis* provides this great ROI, and this is why we're concentrating on this species in this book.

You can, of course, source any of the strains described above, although we recommend sticking to cubes until you're very confident with your mushroom-growing skills. Learning how to adequately grow other strains will necessitate a lot of trial and error, and you need to have a good understanding of the basics before you can change the different parts of your grow properly to accommodate various mushroom species.

Different Types of Mycelial Growth

While learning to grow, you'll become pretty close to your mushrooms; it's impossible to see those little things bursting out into the world without feeling a sense of attachment (or maybe we're just sappy and ridiculous). Over the course of their lives, you'll get to understand and recognize the ways they grow and what proper growth looks like. With this in mind, it's important to know about the two different ways in which the mycelium might appear.

This fluffy tomentose growth will give way to rhizomorphic growth as the mycelium spreads.

Rhizomorphic growth appears to reach outwards from its source on these PF Tek cakes.

Mushrooms will twist and bend themselves into any growing space.

There are two types of mycelial growth: rhizomorphic and tomentose. These two are distinct and look very different, but both will appear in every grow regardless of what species of mushroom you use and what set up you grow it in. Rhizomorphic mycelium growth looks stringy, as if it is stretching outwards, while tomentose mycelium growth looks fluffy and cloud-like. The former will grow quickly while the latter will slowly appear, and while rhizomorphic growth will yield fruits, tomentose doesn't really tend to and will colonize slowly. When growing with the PF Tek method, you may see some tomentose growth on the outside of your fully colonized cakes once you've placed them into the terrarium. This is totally fine, although some growers will confuse the fluffy growth for cobweb mold and freak out. Don't worry if you see this; the tomentose growth will slow and the fruits of the mushroom will start pinning (first emergence from the substrate).

Footnotes

8. Supra note 6 [Stamets, *Gourmet*] at 15.

9. Aldous Huxley. *The Doors of Perception.* 1954. Harper & Row, at 6.

10. Lisa Winter, IFL Science. October 2014. See online: http://www.iflscience.com/brain/magic-mushroom-chemical-hyper-connects-brain.

Chapter 2

Sourcing Your Spores

Which came first: the chicken or the egg? We may never know. Similarly, we'll never know whether the mushroom or the spores came first (don't think about it too long, it hurts), but you're most definitely going to have to get hold of some spores before you can grow any mushrooms of your own.

Spores are the method by which mushrooms propagate. When a mushroom reaches maturity, it spontaneously releases its spores in a cloud of effluvia, much like your average teenage boy. These spores, when released onto a suitable substrate, turn into new fungal growth and eventually into new mushrooms. Once you've got a successful crop of your own shrooms at home, it's incredibly easy to harvest these spores and maintain them for future use—but where can you get your first spores to get you started?

Online

If you've never grown shrooms before and you don't have a friend who is willing to share, your only option is to source spores from a third party.

Most people these days source their spores from online vendors. The Shroomery has a great list of vendor sponsors; these guys do good work and use some of their profit to repay the community that supports them.

Whichever site you choose, be sure to do your own research before buying; the website should have a good reputation, should have good customer service and should have been around for a long time. The more established sites are often the most reliable. There are tons of people online who are keen to take your money and give you nothing in return, so it's worth investing a little time and effort in finding a good spore vendor that won't trick you. Some people will be willing to sell you spores over forums, but we wouldn't recommend this. You don't know who they are, and you don't want to find out the guy typing away to you is actually a cop. Buy from sites that have good reputations and avoid all that.

Spores have been dropped onto this little guy's head!

Spores and the Law

Buying mushroom spores with the intent of cultivating mushrooms is illegal in a lot of countries. Never contact a spore-selling website with any questions regarding cultivation of mushrooms as they will ignore you. This will compromise their security and can put them in a difficult position. The official line, and the one that everyone uses, is that the spores they sell are "for microscopy examination only." This protects the websites from prosecution and helps to protect you as well, although only to an extent. This is a fairly ridiculous dance but one we all have to do. Hopefully when home cultivation of mushrooms is finally decriminalized, we can drop all the nonsense.

We'll show you how to make your own spore prints later in this book.

Try to buy spores from sites that are based in the same country as you. You'll receive your spore syringes in discreet packaging with no indication of what's inside.

All the online security measures mentioned in the introduction apply here. Use a VPN or TOR, make sure your financial and personal information is protected and never get things delivered to the same address as the place you're growing. You can use bitcoin with some sites, which will help to protect your banking information from being tied to your purchase, although many sites still need credit or debit card payments. We won't go over and over this again, but be sure to reread the security section in the introduction properly and take it in; we're not nagging for nothing.

Head Shops

If you live in a moderately large city or an incredibly liberal town, you can also buy mushroom spores in person from head shops, although you shouldn't assume that you can get them from any store that sells cannabis paraphernalia. Do a bit of online research and you might find that there

23

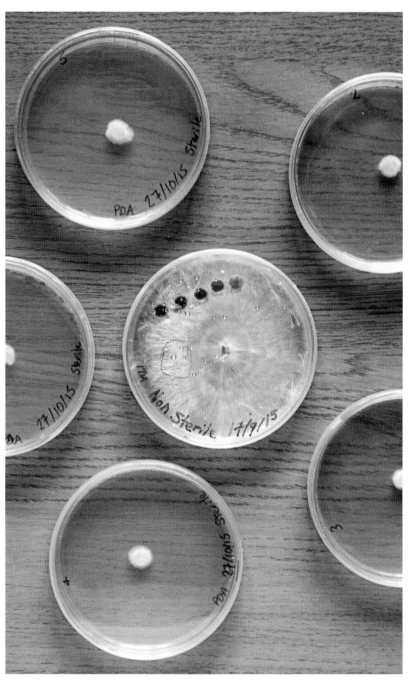

Cloning from tissue is a great way to ensure self-sufficient shroom growing.

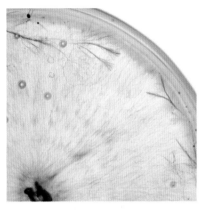

Even contaminated plates of cloned tissue can be cleaned up and used.

This plate is fully colonized and ready to be used!

are a couple of places in your town selling spores. This is actually preferable to buying online, as you can walk in, pay in cash and walk out with your syringes without leaving a speck of information, making it impossible to prove that you ever made the purchase.

As ever, it's difficult to know whether spore syringes from a head shop will be viable, or will even be what they claim to be. We've all been burned before, handing over our hard-earned cash for syringes that likely contained nothing but water, leaving us scratching our heads weeks later when we have nothing to show for it. This will always be a risk when buying spores; the best thing to do is to research the reputation of your local head shops and see which seem to have good ratings from the shroom-growing community.

Pay in cash for your syringes, ensure that the needles are covered, place them deep into your bag and get on your merry way. Don't cruise to your friend's place with spore syringes in your bag, though; go straight home and drop them off. Even if it's not illegal to possess spores where you live, if you get stopped for any reason by the police, having syringes in your bag looks sketchy as fuck. Use common sense.

In the Wild

Our basic recommendation with regard to foraging for spores is this: don't unless you know what you're doing.

In theory, you should be able to find some mushrooms in the wild, identify

This shroom has grown in a restricted space and is malformed as a result.

them as *P. cubensis*, then make a spore print [Chapter 12] or clone [Chapter 10] from them, then use those cultures to grow your own. In theory. In reality, it's difficult, fraught with danger and more effort than it needs to be.

Many people have sourced their spores by foraging for mushrooms in the wild, and that's fine. Many people put mayonnaise on their fries; it's fucked up, but people do it. However, that doesn't mean it's right. If you really want to go searching for *P. cubensis* in the wild, you're going to be hunting through horse shit and mud and soil and more, looking for a very specific type of mushroom that doesn't look all that different from the many other types of mushrooms—and, news flash, some of those types can do you a lot of damage. If you're new to growing, the chances of you correctly identifying *P. cubensis* are little to none, and it's much harder for a newbie grower to start from a spore print or clone anyway. Why not just get a spore syringe and make life a lot easier for yourself? If you use a reputable retailer, your spores will be exactly what they're meant to be, and they'll be handily placed in a syringe that allows for immediate and easy inoculation. There's next to no reason to go looking for your own

A cluster of shrooms at different levels of maturity can drop spores at different times.

when it's this convenient to buy them from a vendor.

However, you might completely disagree with us. If you've been dealing with mushrooms for years, you might feel entirely confident in your ability to spot *P. cubensis* from 100 yards away. Fair enough. Just try to be careful and don't be too obvious while you're on the hunt, and do your research before you head out. There's nothing worse than wasting time, energy and resources on mushrooms that turn out to be psilocybin-free.

From Friends

If you're lucky enough to have friends who are also growing shrooms, you have yourself a fantastic and secure source for your spores. As long as your friend isn't a total blabbermouth and has proven to be security conscious, you can get spores straight from them, and in doing so avoid all the worry about being tracked online or being somehow found out by people who don't need to know that you're growing. Most indoor growers tend to grow *Psilocybe cubensis*, which is the strain we've used in this book, so you're likely to get this type from your friend. If s/he is something of a serious grower, however, you might be lucky enough to get a more uncommon strain, such as *Psilocybe azurescens* or *Psilocybe mexicana.* In this case, take some time out to talk to him or her about the growing methods, dosing and other variables specific to that particular strain.

If your friend is currently growing, you'll be able to get some spores relatively quickly; when mushrooms near maturity, they open their caps and drop their spores. If your friend isn't in the middle of a grow, they may have some spore prints or syringes stored away. Buy them a couple of beers and they're sure to share.

It's super simple to create a spore print, and it's even easier to use that spore print to inoculate a grow; check out Chapter 12 for a step-by-step photo guide on creating and storing your own spore print. We'll also show you how to create a spore syringe, too. Both can be stored for a good long while.

One thing to consider when sourcing spores from other growers is that you can never be sure your spore syringe isn't contaminated or plain dirty. While you can ensure that your own grow methods are sterile, you can't be sure that someone else's are. For this reason, we show you how to isolate spores from a dirty syringe in Chapter 10. Check out the section entitled Purifying Cultures.

Creating a liquid culture is essential for a serious grower.

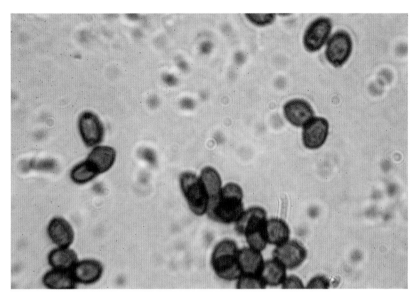

These spores appear dark and egg shaped under a microscope.

Your Own Grow

The absolute best way to source spores is to create a cycle of self-sufficiency. This can start from your very first crop. While spore prints, liquid culture and cloning from tissue are all incredibly successful ways to maintain your spore line, we recommend a combination of all three to ensure the most vigorous mushroom crops and the strongest cultures; we've discussed this in more detail in Chapter 10.

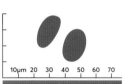

10μm 20 30 40 50 60 70

Spore Scale Bar

● *μm is the symbol for a micrometer, or a micron.*

● *One μm = 1-millionth of a meter, or 1-thousandth of a millimeter.*

● *A typical spore is 11.5-17μm by 8-11μm.*

If you can pull off a successful grow the first time (and with this book, you will be able to), you should only really have to source spores once. Even a moderately successful grow will yield enough mushrooms for you to make a number of spore prints. In fact, all you really need is one spore syringe to start your own liquid culture and this will keep you going almost indefinitely. When you get to grips with agar work as well, all three methods will work towards providing you with viable spores for as long as you want to grow. Ideal!

Chapter 3

Good Practice and Sterile Technique

When growing mushrooms (not just shroom; this goes for any type of fungi), your absolute central concern at all times is going to be cleanliness and sterilization, or rather, the avoidance of contaminants. Maintenance of a sterile environment is what separates the pros from the amateurs in the mushroom-growing game. Once contaminants get inside your grow, it's finished, and you'll have to start all over again with a whole new grow. Repeated instances of contamination, if not dealt with quickly, can increase the number of mold spores in your growing area, leading to a lower chance of success in subsequent attempts.

The better growers amongst us are masters at keeping everything sterile and for that reason can be sure that their crops are always healthy and safe to consume. You should aim to be this type of grower.

Maintaining the good order of your workspace should go without saying, but even (in fact, especially) if you're confident in your methods and have grown successfully a number of times, some of the minor details can slip your mind.

Before you work on your grow, ensure that all the fans and air-conditioning units in your home are off; the room you want to work in should be a

This workspace is a mess, and it's neither safe nor professional.

still-air environment. This gives time for unwanted contaminants to settle. Try to pick a room that doesn't contain a carpet, rugs or other soft furnishings, where mold spores can easily be hidden. A bathroom can be a good choice, as it's easy to spray down with a 10% bleach solution (one part bleach, nine parts water). Make sure you and your work surfaces are clean and before you get started clean your work surfaces with the bleach solution. Wash your hands well and consider using latex gloves to protect your work environment from any contaminants on your hands, especially around your fingernails. Tie up long hair. Surgical masks will protect your grows from contaminants in your breath. Make sure there are no indoor plants around and make sure your pets aren't in the area. Keep all foods away from any growing materials or your workspace.

Glove Boxes and Flow Hoods

Although your workspaces should always be clean and tidy, when it comes to inoculating substrates, cloning, working with live cultures in any way, or handling and using sterilized or pasteurized materials, you should create

Contamination can occur on any medium.

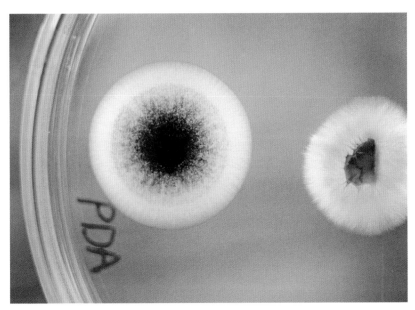

Contamination often outgrows mycelium, ending in something of a standoff and a fight for space and resources!

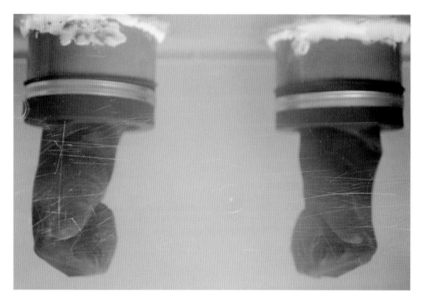

A glove box allows for inoculation in a sterile space.

a smaller, sterile environment to ensure that no contaminants are introduced. By opening a sterilized grain jar in an unsterile environment, for instance, you risk allowing contaminants to settle on the substrate, therefore threatening the success of your entire grow. Sterile spaces are necessary for many elements of mycological work.

If you're lucky enough to have access to proper lab equipment, you'll be able to use a flow hood for many of the processes in this book. A flow hood is an enclosed workbench that takes in air through a high-efficiency particulate arrestance (HEPA) filter designed to remove 99.9% of 0.3 micrometer sized particles. The air is then blown in a laminar flow (in smooth, parallel layers) towards the user, making it difficult for contaminants to settle. Some of these flow hoods also use UV-C germicidal lamps to sterilize the contents of the bench when not in use. However, the vast majority of us won't have access to such a piece of equipment.

Without access to a flow hood, the next best option is a glove box. A glove box is a sealed container that may not have the filters or airflow of a flow hood, but it does provide a separate, enclosed workspace in which to perform mycological tasks. Gloves in the side of the container allow the user to manipulate objects inside. Prior to use, glove boxes are sterilized

This contaminated PF Tek jar must be disposed of properly and with care.

with a bleach solution and offer the mushroom grower a fantastic way to improve the sterility of their grow op. You can buy glove boxes, but we've shown you how to create your own in Chapter 5.

Inoculating in Open Air

Whilst some may see this as a risky option, we've used open-air inoculation with great success. However, this method comes with a number of words of caution. You can't just inoculate wherever you want and not expect contamination.

First find a small room; the smaller the room, the smaller the volume of air in there, and the lower your chance of contamination. It also needs to be easy to clean, so a small bathroom is perfect for this. Close your windows and remove any towels, toothbrushes and toilet rolls—anything that might get ruined by bleach. Use a 10% bleach solution and a cloth to really scrub down the place, taking comfort in the knowledge that all your hard work will impress your friends with your spotless bathroom. Gather your inoculation equipment on a tray: syringes, lighters, liquid culture jars, etc. If you've used a pressure cooker (see Sterilization section in Chapter 6) to sterilize your substrate, keep it closed after cooling and take it into your

Prepping a Still-Air Room

1. If using a bathroom, use the closed toilet lid as your workplace.

2. Scrub the room with a 10% bleach solution and remove brushes, towels, etc.

3. Working through the room from top to bottom and back to front, spray lots of 10% bleach spray into the air.

4. Allow the bleach mist to settle for about 10 minutes, trapping contaminants to the floor.

The advantages of this technique include not being as space-limited as a glove box, which can sometimes be quite tricky to work in. It also gives you more room to do multiple inoculations at once, rather than in batches. However, the disadvantages mean that you have to rehearse the process in your mind and work quickly, just

5. Tie up your hair, wash your hands and get ready to inoculate!

in case there are any rogue contaminants still floating around. This method is particularly suited to syringe-based work (spore syringes, liquid cultures, grain jars / bags), as your exposed areas are kept to a minimum. For methods where you have to physically open your substrate (grain-to-grain, agar work), this method is a lot more risky and you might want to do this work in a glove box, or even better a flow hood.

Keep your workspaces clean and tidy, and remove anything you don't need.

clean bathroom with your other equipment. We normally leave our equipment on the cistern and use the closed toilet seat as our workspace.

Once you have everything set up, take your bleach spray and spray a gratuitous amount of bleach spray into the air, working through the room from top to bottom and back to front. This will help settle out and kill any floating contaminants, and also is why we told you to remove your toothbrush. Move towards the door, closing it behind you, as you spray your way out. Finally, take a towel and seal the gap under the door, leaving the room closed for about 10 minutes whilst the bleach mist settles. Use this time to tie up your hair, wash your hands and get ready to inoculate.

When you go back into the room, open the door slowly so as not to disturb the settled air too much. Then get to work in your clean room, following the photo-essay procedures as appropriate.

Labeling and Your Library System

We're going to get a bit Poindexter here: build yourself a library. We're not kidding. Get used to labeling your stuff and labeling it well. Buy a few fine permanent markers and a hell of a lot of stickers and put them right in

Labeling is absolutely essential for a serious grower.

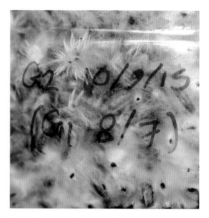

Label jars and bags with the inoculation date and its source.

Working on agar requires good labeling like this.

your grow space. You're going to need them. Good pieces of information to label your jars and boxes with include:

- Date of inoculation—so you can tell how old it is.
- Previous inoculation source (e.g., liquid culture, agar transfer) and the date of the previous source's inoculation. This helps to identify and trace back any sources of contaminants or cultures that are performing badly.
- Substrate / growth medium. Sure you can tell a liquid culture from a grain jar, but label your sugar source (e.g., 4% honey) or grain type to make your life easier.
- Species / strain—only really necessary if you have multiple species / strains.

How a Little Work Can Yield A Lot

Expanding mycelial mass using a combination of liquid fermentation and traditional grain-transfer techniques.

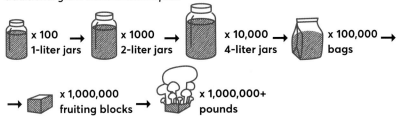

x 100
1-liter jars → **x 1000**
2-liter jars → **x 10,000**
4-liter jars → **x 100,000**
bags →

→ **x 1,000,000**
fruiting blocks → **x 1,000,000+**
pounds

At 1 to 2 pounds of mushrooms per block, more than 1,000,000 pounds of mushrooms can be grown from one petri dish in as short as 80 days, depending on the species and strain. Source: Paul Stemets. Growing Gourmet and Medicinal Mushrooms. *1994. San Francisco: Ten Speed Press.*

Some of you might have dug around and found out about Paul Stamets's P-Value system. This has been a well-known labeling method for a long time. As much as we respect Paul's continued contribution to mycology, we would argue that simply adding an inoculation date to cultures is better, as a simple time-series can tell you far more about the potential state of a culture than the number of times it's been transferred.

If you start trying out lots of different cultures and methods, it's definitely worth getting a notebook. Think of this as your shroom diary, and note down all the work you do, plus any observations; include both what works and what doesn't, the more detail the better. This way you have a semi-quantifiable history of your work, which you can look back over in your more contemplative moments and see if you notice any trends. Are you always getting contamination from one type of grain? It could be that your preparation method needs improving. Are some cultures growing more slowly than others? Maybe you've changed your supplier of grain recently. By keeping good notes on your work, plus a good labeling system, you can create your own personal troubleshooting guide—rather than trusting some guy on the internet to answer your questions.

Chapter 4

Equipment and Supplies

Our goal in this book is to give you enough information for you to make an informed choice about exactly what shape your mushroom grow is going to take. Only you can know how much space you have to grow, what your schedule is like, how many shrooms you need, etc. Our ideal grow might look different from yours, but we hope that we'll help you to build your perfect set up.

Of course, there are some tools and materials that you'll need for every grow. Most of these things can be easily sourced online or in physical stores. In this chapter, we'll take a look at what equipment and supplies you'll need, from the downright essential to the totally optional. Under each heading, we'll start at the necessary ones, then work down to the not-strictly necessary ones .

Where the brand or type of equipment is important, we'll make a note of this for you. For example, the glue that you'll use throughout the growing process needs to be incredibly strong to create the correct seals. Because of this, we've noted the type of glue that we've used as well as an alternative type that will be okay for use if you can't find the recommended brand.

Basic Equipment and Supplies

- Spores (see Chapter 2)
- Syringes and needles
- Silicon injection ports. You can get these easily online.
- Mason / Kilner jars
- Mason / Kilner jar lids
- Alcohol wash
- Tyvek suits / Tyvek arm gloves
- Lab gloves
- Scissors
- Candy (sugar) thermometer
- A scalpel and spare blades

Glass syringes are reusable and come from the best places.

Plastic syringes are single-use only but are super simple to use.

A variety of syringes and sterile needles will be necessary for growing.

Silicon injection ports are worth their weight in gold!

You'll need a variety of lids for different cultivation methods.

Tyvek covers these ventilation ports.

You'll need a scalpel and some sterile blades for a number of processes.

Get a good set of electric scales that can measure small amounts.

You'll need a selection of measuring cups and bowls throughout this book.

An old coffee-grinder will help immensely in your grow.

The strips on autoclave tape turn dark when autoclaved, as seen here.

An Erlenmeyer flask is a conical flask with a flat bottom and a thin neck.

A couple of spray bottles will come in handy, so get one or two!

- Electric kitchen scales
- Pressure cooker
- Autoclave tape. This is an adhesive tape, similar to masking tape, but with strips that change color when the tape has been autoclaved (pressure-cooked).
- Plastic funnel
- Marker pens
- Lighters
- Measuring cups
- Kitchen paper / paper towels
- An old coffee / herb grinder
- A sieve
- A bamboo sushi rolling mat or similar
- Various glass jars, spoons, etc.
- Erlenmeyer flask
- Thick foil
- A plastic sheet or tarp
- Bleach
- Garbage bags
- Elastic bands

43

You can create a fruiting chamber with a reptile tank humidifier.

Equipment for Making Hardware

For the stir plate:

- An old PC case fan
- Two rare earth magnets
- A case of some sort (old cigar box, Lego box, etc.)
- Wire strippers
- Adjustable power source with and adapter
- Wire cutters
- Snap connector
- Speed controller

For the glove box:

- A large plastic tub with lid, 60 liters or larger
- An electric jigsaw or Stanley knife
- Two 4-inch pieces of PVC pipe
- Jubilee Clips
- Heavy-duty rubber gloves
- Silicon sealant
- Sealant gun

For the shotgun terrarium:

- A large plastic tub with lid, around 18 x 14 x 10 inches or larger
- A drill and ¼-inch drill bit

For the fruiting chamber:

- A Martha Stewart portable closet or similar; we'll talk more about this in Chapter 5.
- Measuring tape
- A vise / grips
- Handsaw / hacksaw
- A reptile tank fogger; we'll talk more about this in Chapter 5.
- String / twine
- PVC pipe
- End cap

Some of the more mature shrooms have dropped their spores on the younger ones.

There is some excess vermiculite on the bottom of this harvested shroom.

PF Tek Equipment and Supplies

- Preserve jars
- Brown rice
- Vermiculite
- Perlite

- A spray bottle
- Honey
- Instant coffee
- Gypsum

If you can't get this glue, Loctite Stik'N Seal is a good alternative.

Liquid Culture Equipment and Supplies

- Magnetic stir bar
- Loctite Stik'N Seal / Unibond glue

- Drill and drill bit

Thick foil is an absolute must, especially if you're not using jar lids.

A heat sealer will help you to keep grain bags sterile.

Grain Equipment and Supplies

- Grain bags
- Heat sealer
- Rye berries

- Popcorn
- Birdseed

Syringes, petri dishes and Parafilm will be used throughout this book.

Agar corers aren't essential, but they're super helpful with agar work.

Polypropylene conical tubes are perfect for making agar slants.

Glass petri dishes can be sterilized and reused.

Agar Equipment and Supplies

- Disposable stackable petri dishes
- Glass petri dishes
- Potato dextrose agar powder
- Parafilm
- Tweezers
- Agar corers. These are metal cylinders that allow you to take one piece of agar at a time.
- Polypropylene conical tubes

Bulk Substrate Equipment and Supplies

- Horse manure
- Gardening gloves
- One or two plastic tubs
- An old pillowcase
- A big ol' pan

Always have spare sterile scalpel blades handy and ready to use.

Extraction Equipment and Supplies

- Blender
- Capsule kit
- Gelatin caps
- 70% ethanol
- Dark-glass 20 ml (1 fl oz) dropper bottle
- Dark-glass pill bottle
- Coffee filter
- 75–95% ethanol
- Desiccant sachets
- Knives
- A zester
- A silicon chocolate mold
- A whisk
- Foodstuffs. We've listed these in the breakdown of each recipe.

It's by no means necessary, but if you've got a microscope, it's mad fun.

This dark-glass dropper bottle is incredibly useful.

Dark-glass bottles will help preserve the active material in psilocybin extractions.

Some materials in this book are highly flammable. Be careful!

Packets of desiccant, like silica gel, keep dried mushrooms dry.

You can use 100% silica gel cat litter wrapped in Tyvek as a desiccant.

Chapter 5

Making Your Own Hardware

Mushroom growing is as simple as you want it to be. If you're relatively lazy or short on time and don't want to put in too much effort, you can get by with just some PF Tek jars, but the results won't be great. However, if you're full of energy and want to save time and money, as well as pull off your grow to the best of your ability, you can (and should) make your own hardware with a few cheap ingredients and a tiny bit of elbow grease. In this chapter, we'll show you how.

The pieces of hardware in this chapter are given in order of how necessary they are. For instance, we consider a shotgun terrarium to be essential to pulling off a decent PF Tek crop. You *can* let them grow in the jars, but they won't be fantastic. Rather, you should pop the cakes out into a terrarium and watch them flourish (don't worry if you don't know what we're talking about; we'll cover all this later). If you're unconvinced, flip to Chapter 6 and see the whole method. We'll wait.

See? You need one. It's okay; they're easy to make.

After that, we'll show you how to make your own glove box, or semi-sterile chamber, in which to handle materials. Again, you *could* get away without a glove box, but the potential for exposing your materials to contaminants would be much, much higher. We highly recommend making a glove box; it's not difficult, and it will allow you to gain a more consistent level of sterility throughout. Plus it's fun.

Next, we'll show you how to create a stir plate, which is a little more fiddly. A stir plate will allow you to stir your liquid culture jars without exposing them to contamination. By dropping a magnet into each jar and then placing the jar on top of the stir plate, you allow for the liquid culture to be stirred via the movement of the magnet inside the jar. This breaks up the clumps of culture and encourages further growth. A stir plate isn't necessary, but it's a great tool to have if you are engaging in more intermediate growing methods.

Finally, we'll show you how to build a greenhouse fruiting chamber, which will house your mushrooms in an environment with a controlled humidity. It's really up to you whether or not you want to go down this route; we've found this incredibly useful for growing shrooms in dry weather or in consistently dry locations. While you could construct your own from raw materials, we've found that modifying a store-bought version for your specific use is easier and gives the best value for time and money. However, if you don't feel you need this at all, don't feel too bad about not building one.

We trust you guys to know what's best for you. Just remember to be careful when using tools and dealing with electrics, as losing a finger to a handsaw will ensure the ultimate bad vibe on your next shroom trip.

Making a Shotgun Terrarium

The point of a terrarium is to create a growing environment that mimics the natural ecosystem in which a mushroom would grow outdoors while at the same time ensuring that growth of competing organisms like bacteria and molds are avoided as much as possible. A shotgun terrarium is essentially the cheapest and simplest type of fruiting chamber, and one that's perfect for home cultivation. It doesn't require fans or humidifiers, just a little bit of attention two or three times a day, and it'll yield an impressive crop from PF cakes (see Chapter 6).

The terrarium you'll learn to make in this section is more than adequate for our purposes. It's large enough to contain six PF Tek cakes, and once it's finished and loaded up, it can simply be placed in indirect sunlight and spritzed daily with water. Feel free to make a bigger terrarium if you want to be fruiting more cakes at one time. Some people recommend using humidifiers or artificial light sources with your PF Tek grow. While we've found this unnecessary, it is certainly possible to grow under artificial light. If you do want to go down this route, you'll want to ensure that the bulbs are fluorescent rather than incandescent. Fluorescent bulbs produce light with a color temperature between 5,000–7,000 kelvin, which is the temperature best suited to mushroom growth (daylight sits around 6,500 kelvin, which is why it works so well). One 15-watt bulb in a lamp with the bulb angled towards the side of the terrarium should provide enough light for the type of terrarium we'll be making.

It's also possible to employ a humidifier for use in your terrarium, although we recommend against this as it can create a lot more work than is strictly necessary. The shotgun terrarium we use requires manual misting and fanning a couple of times a day, but we consider this essential; it forces the grower to keep an eye on their mushrooms and means they're more likely to notice any issues early and therefore be able to counter them before anything too bad occurs. The best temperature for growing *P. cubensis* is between 70°F and 80°F (21°C and 27°C) with a relative humidity of 90% or above; this terrarium design maintains a high relative humidity simply with misting and fanning, as the layer of rinsed perlite brings a high moisture content to the set up. If you do choose to use a humidifier, a cool-mist type is best. These can be piped directly into the terrarium and will do away with the need for misting (although fanning, arguably, may still be necessary).

What You'll Need
- *A clear plastic tub with a clear lid. Any size around 18 x 14 x 10 inches will work.*
- *A drill*
- *A ¼-inch drill bit*

In our experience, as long as you grow in the warmer seasons of the year and keep your terrarium in indirect sunlight, there's really no need to complicate the matter by using artificial light and humidifiers. Unless you live in one of those parts of the world where it's pure darkness for six months of the year (in which case inadequate mushroom growth would be the least of your problems), the daylight coming in through your window will be more than enough to grow great PF Tek shrooms. The terrarium design here allows for a humid atmosphere inside without the use of a humidifier. While we'll show you later in this chapter how to construct a greenhouse fruiting chamber that does utilize a humidifier, this is meant for those in drier climates who otherwise may not be able to grow. Otherwise, using artificial lighting or humidifiers raises your costs and increases the risk of fucking

Making A Shotgun Terrarium

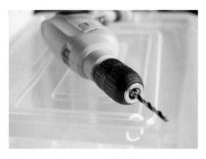

1. Ensure that your drill bit is ¼-inch in size and properly attached to the drill.

2. While drilling, push down gently to prevent cracks.

3. Drill your first hole about 2 inches away from both sides of the lid.

4. Drill the second hole 2 inches away from the first—move your finger first!

up or causing a fire. When the basics work best, stick to the basics.

The theory behind the way a shotgun terrarium works is as follows: Air moves from areas of low pressure to areas of high pressure, and cold air has a lower pressure than warm air. By placing a water-soaked perlite layer on the bottom of the terrarium, we create a cool area of relatively low pressure compared to the air in the chamber above. The area above the perlite is slightly warmer, due to both the respiring mycelium and the heat from the light source, and so is at a relatively higher pressure. A "pressure gradient" is created between the cool air in the perlite and the slightly warmer air above; this drives air molecules from the perlite up into the growing chamber and out of the holes near the top. This serves two purposes:

1. Water vapour in the perlite is mixed with the air and drawn upwards, humidifying the grow chamber. Misting replaces the water lost from the perlite.

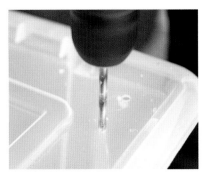

5. Be careful and go slowly. Going too quickly can cause cracks.

6. Continue this pattern, keeping the rows 2 inches apart.

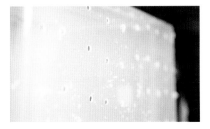

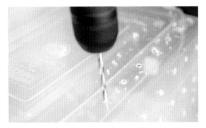

7. When the lid is finished, move on to the sides, keeping up the pattern.

8. Turn the tub over and continue on to the bottom. And you're finished!

2. Carbon dioxide gas, which prevents pinning (fruiting of a mushroom plant), is drawn up and out of the terrarium, encouraging mushrooms to begin forming. Fanning helps drive out any excess carbon dioxide, and refreshes the air in the chamber.

We recommend drilling the one-quarter-inch holes roughly 2 inches apart for the entire top, bottom and sides of the terrarium. We'll be adding a layer of presoaked perlite just before we place the cakes in.

> **Note:** Some growers will tell you that a solid color tub is best here. This is nonsense; light is an important pinning trigger and those growers will often complain about their substandard yields. Clear plastic is far better and will get you a higher yield from your substrate cakes. If you can't get hold of a clear plastic tub (which are widely available and cheap), make sure that at least the lid is clear to allow in some light.

If you want to save yourself some cleanup time, throw a plastic sheet, tarp or any other big bit of plastic underneath your working area before you start drilling. The tiny bits of plastic get everywhere and they're a nightmare to clean up.

Be careful when drilling downwards into plastic. Drill directly from above and let the weight of the drill do all of the work, if you start putting your weight behind it you risk applying too much pressure and cracking the plastic around the holes. One or two cracks here or there aren't too bad, but a few can easily join together and remove whole sections of your terrarium. Go gently. Also, go slowly. The further you get into the semi-tedious process of drilling these things all over your terrarium, the more impatient you'll get, and the more quickly you'll drill the holes. When this happens, you'll drill too quickly and cause it to crack. Then you'll be really annoyed at yourself. Go slowly, take breaks, don't be an idiot.

Throughout this book we've worked in the best possible environment. However, for some methods that should take place within a glove box, we've actually performed the action outside of a glove box to ensure you can see what we're doing (photos inside a glove box tend to be shit). Do NOT rely on the photos to tell you whether or not you should be using a glove box. We will state clearly in the text whether you should be using one or not. For methods that take place outside a glove box, you can rely on the photos to tell you whether or not you should be wearing latex / vinyl gloves. If you see blue gloves ON in the photo, this indicates that you should also be wearing gloves, no exception. If you don't see gloves in the photo, it's up to you—though we recommend erring on the side of caution and wearing them in most situations. If you insist on going gloveless, wash the hell out of your hands and arms up to the elbow, then grab some hand sanitizer and douse those dirty mitts—or just wear gloves.

Making a Glove Box

A glove box is an enclosed chamber that allows you to handle materials in a safer, more sterile or more secure environment. A glove box can be any sort of transparent container of a suitable size with gloves that are attached to the inside of sealed holes on the sides of the chamber. You'll have seen these in labs and in sci-fi movies, or on *The Simpsons* when Homer is at work. The more hardcore of these allow safe handling of radioactive or

Making a Glove Box

1. You'll need all this and a 16-gallon clear plastic tub.

2. Turn the tub on its side and set the plastic piping on the top side, a few inches from the lid edge.

3. Ensure the two pieces of piping are even, then draw around them with a marker.

4. Take the Stanley knife and carefully cut along your marked circle.

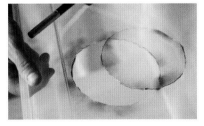

5. If you struggle, heat the plastic sporadically from below with a lighter. *Continues →*

6. If you go too quickly, the plastic may crack like this.

7. However, you can use your hardcore glue to fix such cracks!

8. Push the first piece of piping through one of the holes, ensuring the lip is on the outside of the tub.

9. Using the sealant gun, carefully apply sealant around the piping.

10. Apply sealant all the way around, then gently push the piping to secure.

11. Apply a second layer of sealant, making it neater for aesthetic purposes.

12. Push the second piece of piping through the second hole.

13. Apply the sealant around the piping again, making sure not to leave any gaps.

14. Gently push the piping through the hole.

15. Apply the second coat of sealant as before, keeping it neat and tidy.

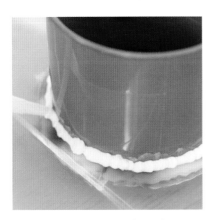

16. Flip over the tub and apply a layer of sealant around the piping inside the tub.

17. Repeat this with the second piece of piping. *Continues →*

18. Ensure that there are no gaps in the sealant. Allow to dry.

19. Take your heavy-duty glove and stretch it over the piping on the inside of the tub.

20. Ensure that when the tub is upside down, your hand will fit in the glove.

21. Put the Jubilee Clip over the glove and onto the piping.

22. Pull the second glove onto the piping, making sure it's correct as above.

23. Pull the second Jubilee Clip onto the piping as shown in the picture.

24. Turn the screw to tighten the Jubilee Clip and secure the glove.

25. Repeat this with the second Jubilee Clip. Ensure the gloves won't come off.

26. Your glove box is ready! Hooray!

otherwise dangerous materials, but for our purposes, a glove box will allow you to safely handle your cultures, out of the way of chance drafts and air currents that might introduce contaminants.

No glove box is entirely sterile, but you should still aim for it to be as well sealed as possible. You can buy these, but they can be wildly expensive and difficult to get hold of, whereas making your own can be cheap, fun and a reason to play with knives.

It's worth making a much bigger glove box than you think you'll need; we've made ones that are just too small before, and it makes it difficult when you're getting to things like grain-to-grain transfer. Also make sure that your gloves aren't too much larger than your hands, as it will make it more difficult to perform delicate tasks.

You'll need a large plastic tub for this (ours is about 16 gallons and is maybe a tad on the small side), as well as some basic tools like an electric jigsaw, though a Stanley knife will do in a pinch. You'll also need some 4-inch pieces of PVC piping, Jubilee Clips that are of a greater circumference than your PVC piping, heavy-duty rubber gloves and some silicon sealant with a sealant gun.

Before you use your glove box, sanitize it by spraying a 10% bleach solution inside and thoroughly wiping it down with a piece of kitchen paper or something similar. Be INCREDIBLY careful with what you use to sanitize the inside of your glove box. While ethanol is great for killing contaminants, spraying a lot into an enclosed space and then flicking a lighter inside to sterilize a syringe is a recipe for disaster. Don't do it. Fire is bad. Check all your cleaning products for flammability, but know that a 10% bleach solution is perfectly safe around fire.

Alternatively, some prefer to simply leave the gloves off the build and do all their alcohol wiping / needle flaming outside the glove box. If you do go down this route, work quickly to avoid contaminants settling on your arms and equipment. You can wear gloves and Tyvek sleeves to protect your chamber from any contaminants on your clothes / hands.

We use a 10% bleach spray and thoroughly wipe down the inside of the glove box, including the gloves. Once you've done this, wipe down your equipment with bleach and place it in the box. As with the sanitized room method, leave everything to settle for 10 minutes, then get to work.

The advantages of the glove box are that it is portable and offers some extra safeguards against contaminants. However, some people find them

Sterilizing a Glove Box

1. Make a 10% bleach solution by mixing one part bleach with nine parts water.

2. With a piece of kitchen paper, wipe down the inside of the glove box with the bleach solution.

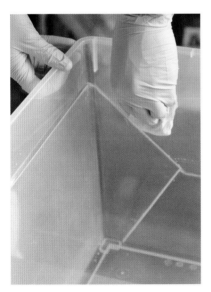

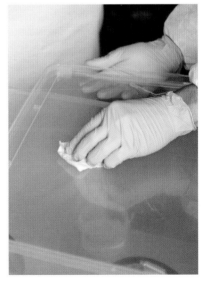

3. Get every single inch of the glove box, including the sides.

4. Don't forget the inside of the lid! Close the glove box and leave it for five minutes before use.

63

difficult to work inside and prefer the freedom of working in a small clean room. Aside from maybe a proper laminar flow hood, no method is completely sterile and you will get the occasional contaminated jar or bag. Factor this into any project and make a few extra jars and be prepared to sacrifice them to the mold-gods. Worst case scenario is you'll just end up with more shrooms than you expected!

Making a Stir Plate

A stir plate will help you to stir your liquid culture after you've sterilized and inoculated it, without opening the jar and exposing the culture to contaminants. Stirring your liquid culture will help break up the mycelium as it grows, preventing it from getting stuck in your syringe when you come to inoculate. Breaking up the clumps of mycelium will also generate many small fragments, each of which can regenerate and quickly grow more. It will also allow for better aeration of the culture, allowing oxygen to be drawn into the liquid to be used by the growing mycelium. A basic stir plate set up involves placing a stir bar inside your liquid culture jar when you're making it, then using a magnet attached to a fan to spin the magnetic stir bar without opening the jar. It's incredibly easy to make a stir plate with a couple of rare earth magnets and an old or cheap PC case fan, which is what we've used.

Making your own stir plate isn't necessary for growing shrooms at home. It's not even necessary if you are using a liquid culture. Some growers use their inoculation syringes to break up the mycelium by repeatedly drawing culture in and out of the syringe. This works, but it's quite difficult to do in a glove box with gloves on. Another method is to put shards of broken glass in your jar before sterilization and then gently shake the jars in the hope that the mycelium will get shredded across the glass, but we really don't recommend this amateur-hour bullshit. However, if you are looking to fine-tune your growing methods and get the best out of your liquid culture, a stir plate is a very good idea. And it's not just useful for mushroom growing; if you, like us, like to brew your own beer as well as grow your own shrooms, it might be worth your while to invest a little time (and not that much money) into making a stir plate. As well as using it for your shrooms, you'll be able to seriously up your home-brew game by making your own brewer's yeast starter and using your stir plate to keep your yeast

Making a Stir Plate

1. Make sure you've got all your equipment ready before you start.

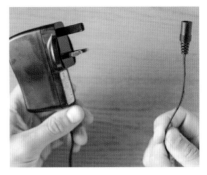

2. This is an adjustable voltage power source with an adapter.

3. Use the wire cutters to remove the adapter; we just need the wires.

4. Split the positive and negative leads a few inches from the end.

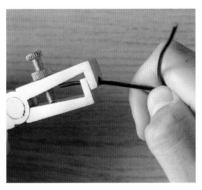

5. Snip off the insulation using wire strippers. Don't go through the wire!

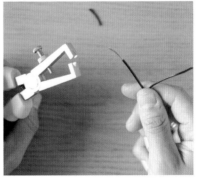

6. Remove about an inch of insulation, not more much.   *Continues →*

65

7. The wire will be frayed. This is normal.

8. Twist the wires by hand to keep them neat and make them easier to use.

9. Twist the ends of both leads; we'll need them both to be neat.

10. Your speed controller will have input and output connectors. Snip the input connector off.

11. If your power source doesn't have an earth wire, separate the earth wire on your speed controller.

12. Tie it off so you know not to use it. It doesn't carry charge so this is safe.

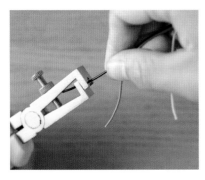

13. Use the wire strippers to snip an inch of insulation off the positive and negative leads.

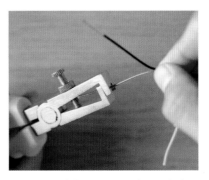

14. Be careful not to cut through the wire! You need it!

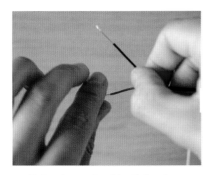

15. Twist the ends of both leads as before. Make sure all wires are contained.

16. Connect positive to negative and negative to positive.

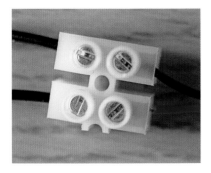

17. Ensure that the wires are properly and safely connected.

18. Connect the speed adjuster to the fan using the snap connector.

Continues →

19. Make sure that your speed adjuster is turned to 12 volts.

20. Turn on the fan to check that it all works. It does!

21. Apply glue to the bottom of your rare earth magnets.

22. Place them onto the middle of the computer fan. Allow to dry for 12 hours.

23. Place the fan into your housing, whatever you're using.

24. Make sure the power source isn't trapped and everything is neat and tidy.

25. Turn it on and make sure that it works!

26. Place your liquid culture jar onto the top and give it a whirl!

27. Try it on a low speed; you should see a whirlpool like this.

28. Try all speeds and see how they affect the liquid culture.

29. The highest speed creates the coolest whirlpool.

healthy while the starter is growing. A yeast starter that's stirred often will yield a higher cell count than one that's not, resulting in quicker fermentation, lower risk of infection and generally better beer in the end. You can also use a stir plate if you've got a hardcore home bread-making game going, though we're more into sourdough ourselves.

If you do want to use a stir plate, you don't have to make your own. They're fairly widely available online for around $60–$100 from all the usual online outlets as well as more specialist mushroom or brewing sites. But if you want to save yourself a whack of money and have a fun afternoon tinkering, make your own. All you'll need is an old computer fan, some sort of case to house it in and some basic tools. We have used the case from an old poker set here, because it's what we had lying around and we like the fact that we can pack it up and take it along with us like a little briefcase. However, feel free to not do this. Anything that creates a bit of space between the magnets and the bottom of the jar is fine. Feel free to get creative; there are plenty of DIY stir plate projects online. Cigar boxes are a good choice if you know someone who enjoys a good stogie, and you can even make it out of Lego if your inner child is waiting to jump out!

While you will be stripping wires and doing some very basic electrical sticking-bits-of-things-to-other-things, we wouldn't recommend doing this if we didn't think it was within the grasp of most of you. However, if you're really not comfortable playing around with wires, ask a friend who might be a bit more confident or buy one online as mentioned above.

Making a Greenhouse Fruiting Chamber

In order to fruit cased-grain or bulk projects, it can be useful to have a greenhouse fruiting chamber. These are often called Martha closets, as the first ones were made from modified versions of the Martha Stewart portable closets from K-Mart. You can buy such greenhouses from most garden centers or from places like K-Mart, and they're simple to put together. Most will fit in your closet. These fruiting chambers maintain their own humidity levels with the help of cool-mist type humidifiers such as the ones you'd buy to put in reptile enclosures. This is a bit of an investment, but they're not expensive and can be completely hidden when necessary. If you're planning on working with larger amounts of substrate, they're fantastic to have.

Making a Greenhouse Fruiting Chamber

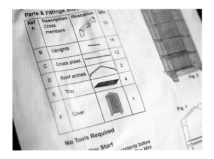

1. You'll need the instructions for your particular Martha closet. Use these.

2. Measure an amount of PVC pipe that will fit the depth of the closet.

3. Carefully saw the pipe according to the mark you've made.

4. If you don't have a woodworking desk, you can set up one like this.

5. Place the PVC pipe against the roof of the closet to check the angle.

6. Mark which portion of the pipe will face into the chamber. We'll drill into this portion.   *Continues →*

71

7. Protect the surfaces that you're going to be working on. Cardboard works.

8. Drill the first hole, being careful not to go through both sides of the pipe.

9. Go along the pipe, leaving about 2 inches between each hole.

10. Many small holes works better than a few large holes.

11. Turn the pipe and repeat this action. Keep the line of holes straight.

12. Stagger the holes so they're placed as in the photo.

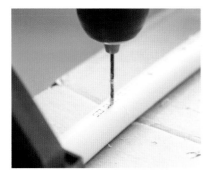

13. Turn the pipe one more time and create a third row of holes.

14. You'll need an end cap to place on the end of your PVC piping.

15. Seal off one end of the tube. You don't have to use a screw end cap.

16. Secure it in place, regardless of what type of end cap you have.

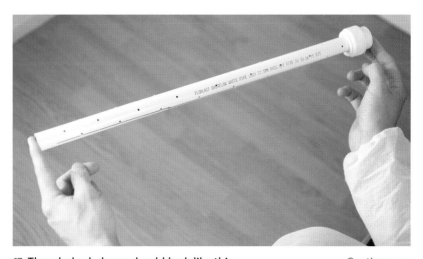

17. The whole shebang should look like this.

Continues →

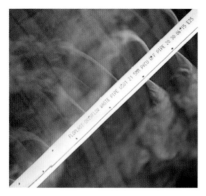

18. Connect the piping to your reptile fogger and ensure that it all works!

19. Build the rest of your Martha closet according to instructions.

20. You may need a beer if this is difficult. We needed several.

21. Place the plastic sheath over your erection.

22. Use scissors or a knife to (carefully) puncture your sheath.

23. Ensure that your pipe fits through the sheath hole.

24. Use wire, string or thread to suspend the diffuser from the closet roof.

25. The back of the diffuser should poke out of the back of the sheath.

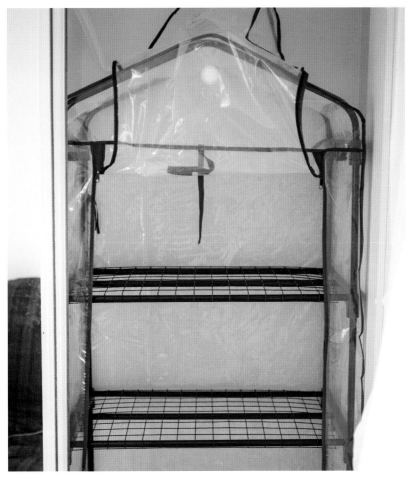

26. Attach the tube of the fogger to the diffuser tube. And you're ready!

Basic PF Tek

PF Tek is your classic indoor mushroom cultivation technique. Like anything, it can be a little tricky to get the hang of, but once you understand the method, it's fairly easy to bring in a good harvest of caps and it's cheap as hell, too. Best of all, it utilizes things that you can get from any supermarket or horticulture shop, so you won't be buying questionable items online or hauling lab gear to and from your apartment.

In this chapter we'll show you how to pull off a successful PF Tek grow from start to finish and also how to get the best out of this grow—including how to bring your cakes to a second flush, getting you two harvests for the price of one. Many growers don't seem to do this, even though it's a total no-brainer.

The Theory

For this one, we've got to thank Psylocybe Fanaticus, otherwise known as Robert McPherson, who popularized and refined this technique (and gave it a name; PF Tek: the Psylocybe Fanaticus Technique) starting in 1991, when it was published in its raw form in *High Times* magazine and so kicked off an entirely new style of indoor mushroom cultivation. The influence that

PF Tek creates a substrate inside a jar, then "births" the jar into a terrarium.

These mushrooms are growing atop a PF Tek cake.

PF Tek has had on growing methods is hard to overstate; it's currently the single most popular indoor growing method, and even if you've outgrown this particular style of growing, it is no doubt the one that you originally used. It made indoor mushroom-growing accessible to almost anyone. Robert (Billy) McPherson passed away in 2011. His contribution to mushroom cultivation will ensure he's not forgotten.

At its heart, PF Tek is really a brown rice substrate method. Brown rice is what will give your mycelium the food it needs; it's what will allow it to grow. However, the addition of vermiculite to the brown rice substrate allows for aeration as the vermiculite pieces add space, forcing the mycelium to stretch to reach the particles of brown rice. This stops the mycelium from forming one huge, dense, impenetrable mass, which is what happens when mushrooms are cultivated on grain alone. Robert McPherson stated that the method was meant to copy nature, in that "mass spore inoculation is employed directly to the fruiting substrate," keeping the genotype intact and maintaining the spores' reproductive capability—in comparison to, say, tissue cloning.[11]

PF Tek cake shrooms can be small, but each cake yields several flushes.

These mushrooms have been picked at the perfect time.

When your substrate has been created, it's then placed into jars with a layer of dry vermiculite to act as a filter (this acts as a barrier between the substrate and the air to prevent contamination), then topped with a lid or heavy-duty foil. These jars are then sterilized, in a pressure cooker normally, then allowed to cool. When the jars are fully cooled, a liquid spore solution is injected through the foil (or pre-drilled holes in the lid) and through the vermiculite layer straight into the substrate, where it germinates and begins to grow into mycelium. The mycelium will eventually overgrow the substrate and pull away from the sides of the glass jar; when they do this, the "cake," as it's known, is ready for removal from the jar. Soaking the cake in water and rolling it in another layer of vermiculite ensures that its water content is maximized, then the cakes are placed into the shotgun terrarium that we made in Chapter 5. Exposure to light encourages the cakes to pin, or to start forming primordia (baby mushrooms), and a humid environment will allow these mushrooms to grow to their full potential. They're picked when their veil is about to break. That's your basic PF Tek theory—and it works.

A dried colonized PF Tek cake. You can see the vermiculite within the mycelium.

Anatomy of a Mushroom

Cap

Mature Mushroom

Margin (edge)

Scales

Gills

Sporophore
(stalk and cap)

Ring (annulus)
Remains of
partial veil

Spores

Stem or Stalk

Universal Veil

Volva Base or Bulb
Remains of
Universal Veil

Fruiting Bodies

Universal Veil

Mycelium

81

This method allows mycelium to completely colonize jars full of substrate.

PF Tek Jars

The type and size of jars used here are somewhat important. The original PF Tek instructions cite Kerr half-pint wide mouth canning jars as preferable for use, but we mostly use half-pint preserve jars with foil on top in-

For this method, you'll need half-pint preserve jars with no "shoulders."

stead. This is because they're slightly cheaper and we've got tons (we eat a lot of preserves). When selecting a jar, look for something slightly tapered and stay away from anything with shoulders (when the top of the jar is narrower than the body). This will ensure that when your cakes are ready to be removed from the jars, all they'll need is a few gentle taps of encouragement and they'll pop right out. If you do accidentally inoculate the wrong type of jar, you'll just have to fruit in the jar (see section Pinning in vitro later in this chapter for some inspiration).

Foil Versus Lids

If you spend a lot of time on mushroom-growing forums, you might see everyone using proper jar lids, whereas we just use foil. Before you start crying charlatan, let us explain. We used to use lids; they got rusty, they got sharp edges from drilling holes, we got tired of losing them, replacing

We use heavy-duty foil, as lids can rust and have sharp edges.

Autoclave tape holds foil on top of the jars and creates injection sites.

them and experiencing the occasional tetanus scare from cut fingers. We use heavy-duty foil now as it's much easier; autoclave tape holds it in place, and the cross of tape provides a perfect area to poke a syringe through without ripping. Use lids if you want, but we love the ease of foil and think you will, too.

Robert McPherson recommended using an ice pick to punch needle holes in your PF Tek lids. We don't recommend this method at all.

Creating PF Tek Cakes

Here's your basic PF Tek recipe. These amounts make one jar.

- 1 jar / cake
- 120 ml vermiculite
- 60 ml brown rice flour
- 55 g water

When mixing your materials, be sure to mix the water and vermiculite before you add in everything else. This ensures that everything else sticks nicely to the wet vermiculite rather than just making one big wet mess.

Creating PF Tek Cakes

1. Ensure that you've got all the ingredients listed in Chapter 4.

2. Pour the brown rice into an old coffee grinder.

3. Grind the rice to a fine powder. This should be fairly easy.

4. Sift the brown rice flour to get rid of any chunks.

5. Measure the right amount of vermiculite into a larger bowl.

6. Add the instant coffee into the water.

7. Stir to dissolve the coffee. Keep going until it's all dissolved.

8. Add the coffee mixture into the vermiculite and stir to combine.

9. Make sure it's evenly distributed and the mixture is evenly wet.

Continues →

10. This is what properly hydrated vermiculite looks like (left hand).

11. Gradually add in the brown rice flour while stirring the mixture.

12. It should look something like this. When in doubt, stir!

13. Add in half a teaspoon of gypsum and stir to combine.

14. Divide the mixture between your jars.

15. They should be filled to the base of the neck of your jars, not right to the top. *Continues →*

16. Make sure that your jars are evenly filled. This will help later.

17. With water, clean the edges of each jar so there are no channels for contaminants.

18. Add a layer of the dried vermiculite to each jar.

19. Fill each one right up to the top.

20. Even off the vermiculite layer. You need to get foil on top.

21. Wrap thick foil over the top of each jar. Make sure each jar is fully covered.

22. Use autoclave tape to secure the foil around each jar.

23. Create a cross of autoclave tape on the top of each jar.

24. This creates four injection sites and also keeps the foil in place.

25. Your jars should look like this! Aren't they great?

26. Place the jars into your pressure cooker. They should sit on a trivet to lift the jars off the bottom of the cooker.

27. Sterilize, and they're ready.

> ### 🚰 A Note on Water Quality
>
> It's easy to find whole swathes of the internet who are concerned about what's in our drinking water. In some cases this concern is justified, but most people living in the developed world have little to worry about. Despite this, many growers swear by using only distilled water in their grows. In our view this is totally unnecessary, and may actually be worse for your cultures; tap water contains many trace elements that are actually beneficial for mycelial growth (e.g., calcium). In an attempt to optimize their yields, some growers may misinterpret genuine information and regard all chemicals as bad. One example of this is magnesium, as a high concentration (<2%) can reduce yields. However this is only an issue when using the wrong type of lime in their casings (see section on Casing in Chapter 9). The typical concentration of magnesium in tap water is around 100 times less than this and poses no practical problems. If you read about a chemical being bad, always check at what concentration it becomes harmful. To borrow an old adage from toxicology, "the dose makes the poison."

Sterilization

Sterilization is a process that uses high temperatures and pressurized steam to kill off any biological contaminants that might be hanging around your substrate. By heating your sample to 250°F (121°C) at a pressure of 15 PSI (pounds per square inch) for 20 minutes, you can effectively kill off any competing molds, bacteria or fungi—leaving all of your substrate for your magic mushroom culture to thrive on.

Commercial growers often use autoclaves or canning retorts to process large batches of substrate in one go. For home growers the best way to sterilize your jars, in the absence of a laboratory-grade autoclave, is a stovetop pressure cooker. These are heavy-duty saucepans with lockable lids and a vent to release pressure when it gets too high. They are capable of reaching the exact same temperature and pressure as an autoclave; in fact 15 PSI was set as the standard pressure for all pressure cookers by the United States Department of Agriculture in 1917. Pressure cookers come in all shapes and sizes, from small and simple with weight-modified valves, to big programmable electric units that can precisely control a variety of settings. Always consult your own care and operating instructions first; pressure cookers can be dangerous if used incorrectly!

To Sterilize Your Jars

Hopefully your pressure cooker came with a trivet—a small metal rack to keep your jars off the bottom of the pan. If not, you will need some way of raising them up off the base, as the direct heat can cause them to crack. A dishcloth will work well for this, but feel free to improvise with whatever heat-resistant material you have around the house. You want your jars to be above the level of water in the pressure cooker, as it's the steam that will be doing all the work to sterilize them. We use about a quart of water in our pressure cooker, which is more than enough to last the 20 minutes of pressure-cooking.

Once the jars are inside, secure the lid in place. Put the pressure cooker on the stove and bring it to a boil. Once the weight starts rocking and you hear the steam hissing out, set your timer for 20 minutes. Once this is done, turn off the stove and allow your pressure cooker to cool completely. Once it's cooled, it's good practice to open it only when you're ready to inoculate. The exception to this is if you have a few batches of jars to sterilize—in that case just store your jars somewhere cool and clean until ready to use (we use the top shelf of the fridge).

These mushrooms have grown from the bottom of a cake and struggled upwards.

Other Methods of "Sterilization"

If you don't want to get a pressure cooker, and you aren't concerned with losing a few jars to contamination, then there are other ways to prepare your jars. The quick and dirty way is simply putting your jars in a pan with a lid (raise them off the bottom as you would for pressure-cooking) and boiling them for 90 minutes. This will kill off most contaminants, but bacterial and mold spores may survive the process.

Another method to get around this is Tyndallization, or fractional sterilization. Named after its inventor John Tyndall, who came up with this technique in the 1800s, this method involves three repeated (usually daily) boiling treatments of 212°F (100°C) for 30 minutes, with cooling in between. The idea behind it is:

- First heating kills any bacteria / mold, leaving behind only spores.
- Second heating kills the spores that germinated since the last heating.
- Third heating kills any remaining spores that the second may have missed.

Whilst Tyndallization is not 100% effective, it's more effective than simply boiling for 90 minutes. However, the daily boiling treatments can considerably slow down your growing project. Also it doesn't work for sterilizing water for making a spore syringe (see section Making a Spore Syringe in Chapter 12), as the spores will never germinate in a nonnutritious medium. For that you will definitely need a pressure cooker.

Cleaning the edges of your jars throughout the process is beneficial.

Autoclave tape secures the foil in place and shows when the jars are sterile.

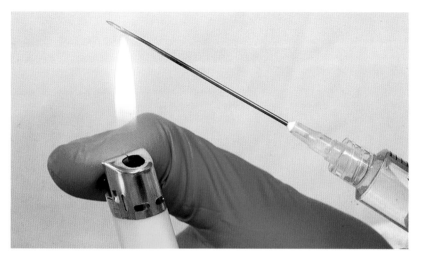

When sterilizing your needle, get the metal to glow red for a few moments.

Inoculation

Don't ever attempt to inoculate your jars before they've properly cooled down. Even if they're only a bit warm don't risk it; they should be cold to the touch.

Some people have success with inoculating PF Tek jars on their kitchen counter, but it's more risky than a well-prepared bathroom (see section Prepping a Still Air Room in Chapter 3) or a glove box (see section Making a Glove Box in Chapter 5). Ideally you should be doing this in a glove box, as it minimizes your chances of contamination.

Once you've acquired some decent syringes from a reputable source, made your own (Chapter 12), or grown your liquid culture (Chapter 7), you're now ready to inoculate your jars. As ever, when handling needles or any other sharps, be careful and don't fuck around; these things are meant to pierce skin, and you don't want to get an armful of *P. cubensis* spores just because you were trying to be funny in front of your growing buddy.

You'll first need to sterilize the end of your needle, for which you'll need a flame of some sort. Normal lighters can be used, but if you've got a blowtorch hanging around your kitchen (maybe you love making crème brûlée? Who knows?) that will be preferable. Carefully remove the needle guard and place it somewhere you won't lose it or knock it onto the ground, then run the end of the needle over the flame of your lighter or blowtorch. The aim is to get the metal to glow red for a few moments; this will ensure

Inject your spores about half an inch away from where the tape meets the edge of the jar.

Inject outwards, towards the glass of the jar. These jars have been inoculated thus.

Condensation on the inside of colonized jars is normal and totally fine.

that it is actually sterilized. If you are working inside a glove box, it's best to do this step quickly outside the box, so as not to accidentally melt the plastic if you're not careful.

When your needle is sterilized, shake the syringe up to disperse the spores throughout the liquid. Insert the needle where the tape meets the edge of the jar; because of the way we've set the tape on top of the jars, there will be four very obvious and useful injection locations. Use them.

When you inject the spores into the jars, inject into these four locations and inject slightly outwards. The tip of the needle should be touching the sides of the glass. This allows the spore solution to slide down the inside of the jar and will create more inoculation points down the side of the sub-strate. When the mycelium starts to grow, it will strangle the medium somewhat and pull the medium away from the glass, meaning that there will be a space between the grain and the glass. This will allow condensa-tion to form there. Don't worry about this at all—it's a good sign!

You want to use around 2cc of spore solution per jar, so when you've used around a quarter of this, remove the needle from the first injection point and move on to the second. Repeat this process until you've injected 2cc into the jar through the four injection points.

If you're working with liquid culture instead, the procedure is mostly the same, except you need to draw up your liquid culture into a sterile sy-ringe first. If you use a fresh needle and syringe straight out of the pack, you won't need to flame sterilize before drawing up the liquid culture. Give the culture a quick stir to break up any clumps of mycelium, then move it into your glove box and use the syringe to draw up as much as you need. You might need to do this a few times if you have a lot of jars, so make sure you flame sterilize the needle in-between.

Once your jars are inoculated, place them in a warm, dark place to colo-nize. We favor an airing cupboard for this, but anywhere that's dark will do. Place the jars on a high shelf if possible, as this will keep them away from the contaminants that exist at floor level and get whipped up every time someone walks by. As we've already discussed, the growing season in your location will be from late spring to early fall, so the temperatures should be suitable for mushroom growing during this time. An ambient room tem-perature of about 70°F (21°C) is best. If it's too cold, your mycelium simply won't grow.

This is the first sign of colonization a few days after inoculation.

The mycelium will spread outwards from the injection sites and meet.

These PF Tek jars are at different stages of mycelial growth.

The mycelium will overwhelm the substrate, even at the bottom of the jar.

Colonization should begin within a few days of inoculation with spores, or within 24 hours if you're using liquid culture. The first thing you'll notice will be the fuzzy white spots appearing on your substrate; these are germinating spores.

More of these will appear and during the next four weeks, they'll grow and grow, hopefully exhibiting rhizomorphic growth, which is exactly what we want. As these rhizomorphs grow together, they'll create a white covering over the entire substrate and will eventually begin to strangle the substrate and pull it away from the sides of the jar. This is perfect, but it can allow space for some moisture to gather on the glass. Don't worry if this happens; it's perfectly normal.

Deciding When They're Ready

Once the substrate inside your jars is fully colonized, including the bottom of the substrate, give them about another week before removing them from

Rhizomorphic growth away from the injection site is perfect.

the jars. This allows the mycelium to consolidate, meaning it will move into fruiting more quickly once placed in your terrarium.

Depending on how long you've left your jars, you might be able to see the beginnings of the mushroom fruit (the primordia) snaking their way along the inside of the glass; in fact, Psylocybe Fanaticus recommends waiting until these primordia are showing before transferring your cakes to the terrarium. They'll look like tiny worms with darker colored spots on the ends, sort of like angry baby eels.

Prepping the Terrarium for the Cakes

When your cakes are entirely inoculated and pulling away from the sides of the jars, you should start preparing your terrarium. If you're doing the dunk and roll, as we recommend, you can prep the terrarium while the cakes are soaking overnight. However, if you're not doing the dunk and roll, you'll need to prep the terrarium before you pop the cakes out of their jars. Cakes shouldn't be left out of their jars while you finish all your business.

You should have your terrarium already made, but before it's ready to host cakes you'll need to fill it with a few inches of rinsed perlite to help create the pressure gradient that will draw fresh air into your terrarium

The jars are fully colonized and ready for the terrarium!

and ensure good passive ventilation. When you fill the terrarium with the rinsed, cold perlite, you'll create an area at the bottom of the terrarium with a lower temperature than the rest of it. The air above the perlite will stay slightly warmer due to its exposure to light. This small temperature differential will create a pressure gradient, and as air currents flow from areas of high pressure to areas of lower pressure, this will draw air up into the terrarium, through the perlite and into the chamber of the terrarium. This air will eventually escape the terrarium through the holes in the lid, taking with it the CO_2 created by the mycelium. This process ensures great ventilation, minimizing how often you need to fan out the stale air.

Rinsing your perlite is incredibly simple; either cut holes in the bottom of your perlite bag or tip the right amount of perlite into a colander and run cold water through it for a couple of minutes, then allow it to dry out slightly. We don't recommend rinsing the perlite when it's already in the terrarium; although most of the water would run out of the holes at the bottom, it opens up the possibility of standing water, which is never good. Once water is no longer dripping from the bottom of the bag or out of the colander, spread the perlite along the bottom of the terrarium. It should at least cover a couple of inches up from the bottom. Spread it out so it's as even as possible.

Prepping Your Shotgun Terrarium

1. Cut three holes in the bottom of your perlite bag with a large knife (careful!).

2. Cut another large hole in the top, opening it up.

3. Run cold water through the perlite bag, soaking it all.

4. Keep the water running through the bag for several minutes.

5. Lift the bag and allow the excess water to run out. Leave it to drain for a few minutes.

6. Pour the rinsed perlite into your pre made shotgun terrarium.

7. Flatten the perlite so it creates an even floor.

8. Tear off some thick foil to make a base for the PF Tek cakes to sit on.

9. Fold into squares. Create as many squares as PF Tek cakes.

10. Place foil onto your even layer of rinsed perlite with space in-between.

Birthing Your Cakes

1. Before you handle the cakes, wash your hands thoroughly.

2. We said thoroughly. Go on, wash them again. They still look dirty.

3. Remove the foil and autoclave tape from one of the jars.

4. Use your fingers to gently remove the vermiculite layer.

5. Turn over the jar into the palm of your hand and slap it firmly with your other hand.

6. Keep going until the colonized cake comes away from the jar and falls into your palm.

7. Remove the jar entirely and admire your handiwork. You grew that!

8. Turn over the cake and wipe away any remaining vermiculite from the top of the cake.

9. Set down the clean cake in a safe and clean place.

10. Remove the foil from the next jar and repeat.

11. Clean any erroneous bits from the cakes as you go.

12. Once all your cakes are "birthed," you're ready to soak them.

Birthing Your Cakes

When it's time to remove your cakes from their jars, undo the foil tops, get a tray to catch all the vermiculite and tip the jars out into it. Turn each jar upside down and tap firmly on the upturned bottom of the jar until the cake starts to come out. Keep going until the whole thing comes out of the jar, making sure you're as gentle as you can possibly be; you don't want to manhandle the poor little things. Once they're all out, you're ready to move on to the next step.

The Dunk and Roll

This is an essential step if you're planning on maximizing your final yield, and it's as easy as it sounds. The theory here is that because mushrooms are almost 90% water, and because the water in a cake runs out before the nutrients do, soaking the cake in water will allow more mushrooms to

Man overboard!

Someone save him!

No? No one?

grow, increasing your yield. It will also allow you to easily harvest two or even three big flushes from the same cake, meaning you can get way more mushrooms for almost no more effort.

This is a two-step process, as after the dunk, you'll roll your soaked cakes in dry vermiculite. This will make the vermiculite stick to the outside of the cakes, which in turn will increase their water-retaining capabilities.

The "dunk" portion of this process is simple: get a clean, large bowl, fill it with cold water and gently place your cakes into it. Use something to ensure that the cakes aren't bobbing up at the top of the water level; we've found that using a small plate to weigh them down keeps them all underwater and doesn't cause a mess. When the cakes are weighed down, place the whole shebang into the fridge and leave it for 24 hours.

Fresh, fully colonized cakes are pretty contamination resistant and vermiculite is nonnutritious, so feel free to use dry vermiculite straight out of the bag. But if you're extra careful like we are, you can bake your vermiculite in your oven to dry-sterilize it. While your cakes are soaking, prepare the vermiculite that you'll use to roll the cakes in. To do this, place your vermiculite (about one cup per two cakes) in a clean oven dish, cover in foil

Soaking Your PF Tek Cakes

1. Fill a large bowl full with cold water. Tap water is fine.

2. Rinse one of the PF Tek cakes under the cold tap for several seconds.

3. Gently set the first cake into the bowl of water.

4. Repeat the steps with the remaining cakes, rinsing off any bits and pieces.

5. Set all cakes into the water. You'll notice that they float.

Continues →

6. Get a plate that's smaller than the circumference of the bowl and wash it.

7. Front and back. Go on, we'll wait.

8. Gently set the clean plate on top of the cakes.

9. Allow the plate to pin the cakes under the water level.

10. Cover the bowl with Saran Wrap and set it in the fridge for 24 hours.

Drying the Vermiculite

1. Pour your vermiculite into an oven-proof baking tray or ceramic dish.

2. Even out the vermiculite and cover with foil.

3. Ensure that the dish is completely covered. Preheat the oven to 350°F (177°C).

4. Place into the oven and bake for one hour. Allow it to cool before use.

and put in your oven, preheated to 350°F (177°C), for one hour. Keep covered and make sure it's fully cooled before use.

The next day, remove the bowl from the fridge and grab your vermiculite.

Spread the vermiculite in a shallow dish or tray, or just use the one in which you baked it in if you pre-sterilized it. Remove one cake from the water and rinse with cold water, making sure that there's nothing erroneous clinging to the outside. Once you've rinsed it well, place it on its side at one end of the tray and roll it in the vermiculite, ensuring that all the sides are covered. Place upright and sprinkle some vermiculite on the top, making sure there's full coverage. Set aside and repeat with the rest of the cakes.

Once your rolled cakes are in your terrarium, give them about 30 minutes before wetting them. This allows the dry vermiculite to passively absorb some of the moisture and stick better to the cakes. When you do spray

Rolling the Cakes

1. Remove the soaked cakes from the fridge and fish out of the water.

2. Rinse each cake under cold water for a minute or so.

3. Place one cake on its side into the dried vermiculite.

4. Gently roll the cake in the vermiculite so it is completely covered.

5. Stand the cake on its end and drop some more vermiculite onto the top.

6. Place the rolled cake onto a foil square inside the terrarium.

7. Repeat the process with each of the soaked cakes.

8. Ensure that the sides, top and bottom are all covered in vermiculite.

9. Place each cake onto a foil square. Ensure that they're stable.

10. Lightly spray water outwards, onto the sides of the tub.

When spraying water into your terrarium, spray the inside walls of the terrarium. Don't spray the cakes directly.

your terrarium, don't aim directly for the cakes, as this will blast off the vermiculite; instead mist gently around them. If you've put additional vermiculite on top like we did, you can add a little bit of extra moisture to this with a teaspoon or two of water.

You can, of course, skip this step if you really want to, or if you can't get hold of any more vermiculite for some reason. If this is the case, we still recommend the dunk without the roll. We've pulled off a terrarium grow like this before but the resultant mushrooms tend to be malformed and don't grow as rapidly or in as great numbers. Without rolling, your yields will be lower and your mushrooms not as pretty, but you'll still have a good batch of mushrooms at the end of it, so if you can't get hold of enough vermiculite to make this happen, it's not the end of the world.

Into the Terrarium

When it's time to move your cakes into the terrarium, you'll want to set your cakes on small squares of foil (or your jar lids if you went down that route) to prevent the mycelium growing into the perlite in a pointless search for more nutrients. Use thick foil and fold into squares slightly larger than the circumference of your cakes. Place the squares relatively close together in the middle of the terrarium and then place one cake onto each. It's actually better to have six or more cakes inside this size of terrarium, as slightly crowding it helps the mushrooms to grow, but we've successfully grown with just three inside, as you can see from the photos.

A cluster of mushrooms appears on the top of a PF Tek cake.

Set your terrarium ideally on a table or desk (to keep it away from all those pesky contaminants at floor level), and set it on something that will allow for airflow underneath it. It only needs to be lifted up about an inch for optimum airflow to occur. Four equal-sized glass jars or even Solo cups are perfect for this; just put one underneath each corner and be careful not to knock it over as you go by it. Light is an important pinning trigger, so your cakes will need sunlight to sprout. Indirect sunlight is best, so place the terrarium not directly in front of a window but perhaps next to a wall across the room or against the wall perpendicular to the window. White walls will reflect light and help your mushrooms to grow.

It's important to mist your terrarium with water several times per day. You can do this as little as twice per day, or as often as you see fit. We've noticed a definite improvement in the size and vigor of the mushrooms with increased spritzing, but don't go nuts and make the inside of the terrarium too wet; you don't want to have water dripping out of the bottom. Some growers talk about hygrometers here as a way to ensure your desired

111

humidity is maintained, but the truth is that inside a terrarium it's going to be near impossible to get a decent reading without expensive hygrometers and you've then spent money on a near-useless and unnecessary piece of kit. When it comes to mushrooms, the increased yield you'll get from such a process is negligible anyway; keep things simple and consistent. This terrarium is designed so that the humidity is adequate for growing. Don't feel like this is something you need to obsess over. Get a spray bottle and keep it by your terrarium. Two to three times every day, remove the terrarium's lid and spray water onto the inside walls of the terrarium; don't spray the cakes directly. We spray around 20 times, then gently waft the air to get rid of some of the CO_2 and excess humidity. Pop the lid back on and leave them to do their thing.

The Fruiting Period

It won't take long for your cakes to start fruiting. As light is a pinning trigger, they should start to pop out from the vermiculite within a couple of days of being placed in the terrarium, as long as the terrarium is exposed to light.

You'll notice that your cakes look a little blue when they're in the terrarium, and inexperienced growers might freak out thinking that this is mold. Don't worry; this bluish tint is a result of the cakes being handled, and it's perfectly normal. If the color starts to deepen and spread, then you may have an issue on your hands, but at this point the likelihood of mold taking hold is low. Your first little flush of mushrooms might look odd and misshapen, but don't worry; this is also pretty normal. In some areas you may get clumps of mushrooms that start to grow, but then never get bigger. These are affectionately known as "aborts" by some growers, and though they look unappetizing, they're actually pretty potent and are totally safe to pick. The more traditionally shaped mushrooms will come a few days later, and when they spring out, boy do they spring. Your mushroom fruits will grow in clusters and will also grow on the underside of the cake, tipping the cake over slightly.

The vigor of *P. cubensis* when they're grown this way is a sight to behold; once your little shrooms have popped, they'll reach right for the stars. Don't worry if your mushrooms aren't exactly uniform in size; most likely they're going to be a diverse little bunch, some huge and some relatively squat and fat. They're all good, so let them grow to their capacity, then pick them.

Your mushrooms will grow so rapidly that you'll love to watch them.

The first mushrooms are popping out of the cakes! Aren't they cute?

Your shrooms may grow unevenly. This is totally fine!

Harvest

While it's tempting to just let your mushrooms grow and grow forever, they're not built that way—and they'll let you know. When the caps of your *P. cubensis* unfurl and spread out, you'll be able to see the veil that stretches from the stipe to the edge of the cap. This veil covers the gills, and therefore the spores. When a mushroom reaches maturity, it stops expending energy on growing and instead focuses on dropping spores to ensure that its genetic line can continue; when it's preparing to drop spores, the veil will begin to tear away and curl up into itself.

There's some discussion about when to harvest mushrooms for optimum potency. Some say that it's best to harvest the fruits just before the veil breaks; this is obviously difficult to time if it's your first grow, but once you've pulled off a couple of harvests you'll get to recognize the subtle signs that your mushrooms give you, and you will get used to harvesting them at the desired time.

These tenacious little mushrooms are unbalancing this cake.

Mushrooms may sprout from the bottom of the cake, tipping it over slightly.

The veils on these mushrooms have torn, and they're ready to be harvested.

Harvesting

1. Put on your latex gloves and spritz them with alcohol.

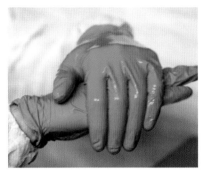

2. Rub the alcohol all over, ensuring you cover every bit of the gloves.

3. Allow the alcohol to dry. This should take a minute or so.

4. Place your thumb and forefinger at the base of the mushroom and twist.

5. Lift the mushroom gently away from the cake; it should come away easily.

6. Set the mushroom aside and repeat with all the mature shrooms.

117

The harvested cakes will be blue and relatively dry. This is nothing to worry about.

If you miss the tearing of the veil (which sounds a lot creepier than it is), don't worry; you'll soon notice that your mushrooms are ready to be picked because they'll dump their spores and all of a sudden the cakes and the perlite on the bottom of the terrarium will be covered in a blue-purple-black powder that appears first in very distinct lines, and later in a mess of patches. Yes, it looks cool as hell but it's a sign that you should have picked your mushrooms sooner. No biggie; just pick them as soon as you notice the spores. After they drop spores they'll start to wither. They're past their prime.

If you want to harvest your mushrooms earlier for any reason, this is totally fine. The remaining nutrients in the cakes will simply be redirected towards new unharvested mushrooms, so don't worry about anything going to waste.

Once your mushrooms are ready, gently take the cakes out of the terrarium and pull each mushroom off, one at a time. Place your thumb and forefinger right at the base of the mushroom and simply break it off with a little twist; they should be fairly easy to remove. Weigh the harvest (if you want to keep track of your yields) and set the cakes aside. You can bring these to a second flush, so don't throw them away.

After the first flush, resoak the cakes for 24 hours. However, do NOT roll in vermiculite.

Place the mushrooms onto a slatted surface so that they can dry evenly. We have found that a sushi-rolling mat works really well for this. We've written a whole chapter about drying and another about how to consume your harvest; flick to Chapters 12 and 13 to read more on this.

From inoculation to harvest should take around six to eight weeks.

The Second Flush

When you've picked your cakes free of mushrooms, it's time for the second soak and flush. That's right; those bad boys can be used all over again for another harvest. Don't throw them away!

Once your cakes are clean of mushrooms, it's time to rinse them and soak them once again, as shown above. Don't do the roll part of the dunk and roll this time, however; once they've been soaked, you can pop them straight back into the terrarium and watch those bad boys fly once again. The rationale behind not rolling is that to do so would trap any contaminants that may have landed on the cakes during the flush. While you've been spraying and fanning and taking a million photos of your grow, you've most likely been letting particles of who knows what into the terrarium. While these will sit on the outside of the cakes and be somewhat harmless,

On subsequent flushes, more shrooms will grow underneath the cakes due to pooling water.

it's been argued that a new layer of vermiculite would "protect" these con-taminants, allowing them to germinate and totally fuck up your cakes. You don't need another layer, so why take the risk? Simply dunk and place into the chamber. Easy as pie.

While your second lot of shrooms is growing, the cakes may seem to have more of a bluer tint than the first time. This is most likely to be bruising, as the cakes have, at this point, been handled quite a lot, and their resistance to bruising is lower. However, you should keep an eye on this, and if it spreads, it is likely to be mold. In this instance, the affected cakes should be thrown away; it's time to start again. No exceptions.

You may notice that the shrooms grown in your second flush seem to be more oddly shaped than the first and growing in more dense clusters. This is normal, and tends to be hilarious if you're somewhat immature. You'll also notice more mushrooms growing from the bottom of the cakes—or at least that's been our experience. This may be due to water pooling inside the cakes at the bottom. If your mushrooms or cakes appear to be more blue than normal, this could be an indication that they're drying out.

A yield that's roughly three-quarters the weight of your first is about

If you dry out your harvested cakes and break them up, you can extract psilocybin from them. We'll show you how.

average for a second flush. The second flush isn't always the end of the road for your cakes, either. Some growers report getting third and even fourth flushes out of their cakes, although the yield will diminish every time. However, if you can keep encouraging those cakes to fruit, then why not? Unless you're desperate to fill the terrarium with all-new cakes, we say it's worthwhile. Even after your final flush, it's not time to throw your cakes away; in Chapter 13 we'll tell you how to extract psilocybin from your cakes to squeeze every last drop out of every PF Tek grow.

Pinning In Vitro

If you don't want to go through all these stages of PF Tek, you can actually allow your cake to pin in vitro; that is, you can let them start growing the fruit of the mushrooms while they're still inside the glass jar. This removes the terrarium from the method, meaning that you won't need to dunk and roll or anything after that. Even if you do plan on transferring your cakes into a terrarium, they will start pinning in vitro regardless if you leave them for too long, as mycelium wait for no one. While most growers will remove their cakes from the jars at the first sign of in vitro pinning, other growers may prefer to keep them in the jar for the entire growing process—until the mushrooms are fully grown. This will result in bent and contorted mushrooms, but if you don't care what they look like and have other concerns that make in vitro pinning a good choice for you, then feel free to simply leave your cakes where they are. For instance, some growers who still live with their parents, or at college, or with non-psychonaut roommates may not want to bring their grow out into the open by using a terrarium, which is admittedly hard to hide. In this instance, it would be preferable to keep the grow as discreet as possible; after all, PF Tek jars take up almost no room, and as long as they don't become contaminated, they should be fine when left for a while. However, if you are hiding your cakes from someone or something, remember that they will need exposure to light in order to pin and grow, so don't just shove them under your bed and expect to get mushrooms at the end of it. If you're a terrarium grower normally but you're going on vacation around the time that your cakes would be ready for the terrarium, or if you're not going to be home enough to tend to a terrarium but don't want to lose out on the growing time, then this could be a good option for you. We've heard this called Neglect Tek

This cake has been allowed to pin in vitro. This is not ideal.

before, and we sort of love that.

Of course, restricting the space that your mushrooms have to grow into will eventually mean that their growth is stunted and the weight of your yield will be lower. One real concern, though, is that in vitro pinning will leave your mushrooms covered in vermiculite, which necessitates either picking them clean or extracting the psilocybin via alcohol or in a tea (Chapter 13). They can be eaten as long as you make sure there's no vermiculite left on them at all.

To get a little emotional for a second, it's absolutely beautiful to watch your mushrooms grow when you've followed the full and proper PF Tek method. They seem to spurt by the hour; if you set up a camera on a time-lapse you'll actually be able to watch them. A little cap poking through the vermiculite in the morning can be a hefty shroom by the time you go to bed. Those who think that growing mushrooms can't be just as spiritual an experience as growing cannabis have never watched a handful of *P. cubensis* caps emerge from a freshly prepared cake; seeing those little shrooms make their way into the world will make your Grinch's heart grow three sizes.

Footnote

11. Fanaticus, April 2010. See online: http://www.fanaticus.com/intro.htm

Chapter 7

Liquid Culture

One of the best and simplest ways to expand your grow and move on to more intermediate techniques is to get to grips with liquid cultures.

As the name suggests, a liquid culture allows propagation of a mycelium culture in liquid form, which then allows for inoculation of a growing medium via syringe. Basically, we're talking about mycelium suspension in some sort of sugar solution. Good quality spore syringes usually contain sterile water, in which thousands of dormant spores are suspended. This is known as a multispore suspension. For spores to germinate into mycelium in a liquid culture normally takes between three to seven days. This means your subsequent inoculations will "hit the ground running," quickly penetrating the medium before any contaminants can gain the upper hand (though if you follow the proper sterile techniques in this book, that shouldn't be a problem). For home growers who want to take their set up to the next level, liquid cultures are invaluable as they allow you to turn a little inoculating medium (dormant spores) into a lot of inoculating medium (actively growing mycelium), saving you time, money and a lot of effort in the long run. The good news is that they're not difficult to make either.

Once you've sourced a single spore syringe, you can use the methods

A liquid culture will give you a near-constant supply of these. Seriously.

below to make much more mycelium-infused liquid, keeping the culture going as long as you need to. We'll show you how to make a Mason jar suitable for liquid culture growth and storage, how to use a stir plate (the one that you made in Chapter 5) to help you agitate and therefore mix cultures in the liquid without contaminating it, how to make the liquid culture itself and how to sterilize it without caramelizing the sugars in the medium. Once you have made the liquid culture jar, sterilized it and inoculated it with sterile spores, you can be sure that every time you use that culture, it will be sterile

and active. When you have to buy spore syringes time and time again, this isn't always the case; all home growers know the pain of the spore syringe that just didn't yield anything. That sucks, so let's avoid it.

Another benefit of making and maintaining your own liquid culture is that you heighten the security around your own mushroom-growing operation. Buying spore syringes online always carries with it the possibility of getting caught; no one wants this. Dealing with unscrupulous vendors isn't fun, and there's no guarantee when you send your money down the international information superhighway that some real spores are going to arrive at your door. Add to this that the spore syringes aren't cheap and most definitely

Honey

Nutritional Value per 100 g (3.5 oz)

Energy	1,272 kJ (304 kcal)	
Carbohydrates	82.4 g	
Sugars	82.12 g	
Dietary fiber	0.2 g	
Fat	0 g	
Protein	0.3 g	
Vitamins		
Riboflavin (B2)	0.038 mg	3%
Niacin (B3)	0.121 mg	1%
Pantothenic acid	0.068 mg	1%
Vitamin B6	0.024 mg	2%
Folate (B9)	2 µg	1%
Vitamin C	0.5 mg	1%
Minerals		
Calcium	6 mg	1%
Iron	0.42 mg	3%
Magnesium	2 mg	1%
Phosphorus	4 mg	1%
Potassium	52 mg	1%
Sodium	4 mg	0%
Zine	0.22 mg	2%
Other Constituents		
Water	17.10 g	

Shown in for 100 g, roughly 5 tbsp.

Source: Wikipedia

aren't legal and it's obvious to see that keeping your own liquid culture is preferable.

Creating a liquid medium for spores to germinate in isn't difficult, and it only requires a few cheap ingredients. Unlike plant seeds, which possess a small amount of starter nutrients with which to begin growing (known as an endosperm), mushroom spores require sugar to begin their germination process inside the liquid medium. You can use almost any type of sugar for this. Household sugar (sucrose) or pure dextrose should be avoided, as they lack the additional elements that promote healthy mycelial growth. You can, however, use Karo, light malt extract, corn syrup or maple syrup, but our choice of sugar is honey, as this has natural antibacterial qualities, is cheap and widely available, and dissolves nicely into water. Whilst nutrient profiles can vary a lot between producers, typical honey is a mix of: simple sugars; monosaccharides such as glucose (31%) and fructose (38–55%); disaccharides such as maltose and sucrose; a few other more complex sugars; vitamin B and C; and minerals such as potassium, calcium and phosphorous, which are essential for healthy mycelial growth.

Once the honey is mixed with water and inoculated, it takes only a week or so for a good amount of culture to grow. Stirring helps to shred the initial clumps of mycelium, creating hundreds of new fragments that can each regrow into new individual colonies. As the mycelium grows over time, it will deplete the sugars in the solution and eventually enter

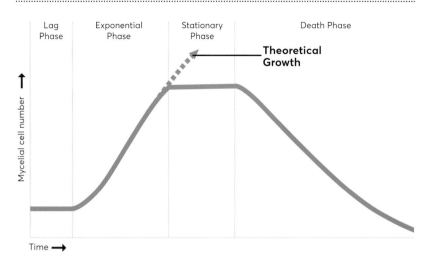

| Lag Phase | Exponential Phase | Stationary Phase | Death Phase |

Theoretical Growth

Mycelial cell number ↑

Time ➜

Typical growth curve for mycelium in liquid culture. Source: Wikipedia/Creative Commons

the stationary phase. When it reaches this stage, it can be stored in the fridge for later use. It is worth noting that cold, stationary phase cultures will slowly lose their vigor (i.e., their ability to quickly regrow) over time, but we have successfully kept a regrown liquid culture for up to a year with no problems!

To start, though, we need a receptacle for the liquid culture that can be kept sterile while allowing us to inoculate and to stir the liquid inside. No problem.

Making Liquid Culture Mason Jars

Equipment:

- A drill and drill bit
- A 16 oz Mason jar
- A stir bar
- Scissors
- Unibond Extreme Repair Glue / Loctite Stik'n Seal
- A silicon injection port
- Two small pieces of Tyvek

Note: You can source silicon injection ports fairly easily on sites like Amazon or in medical supply stores. They're inexpensive and don't tend to bring you any unwanted attention from the internet police, though as mentioned before we would recommend using something like a VPN if you're planning to buy anything dodgy online.

Making a Liquid Culture Mason Jar

1. Ensure that your equipment is ready and your drill is working and safe.

2. Place a magazine or phone book on your table. Gently drill a hole in your lid.

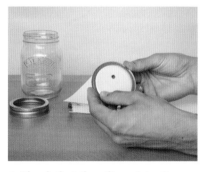

3. Go all the way through, then gently lift the lid off the drill bit.

4. Check that the silicon injection port fits the hole. Don't push it through yet.

5. Repeat the action to create a second hole about an inch from the first.

6. Ensure that the holes are centered and well spaced.

7. Cut two square pieces of Tyvek to completely cover one hole.

8. Glue around one hole with your super-powered glue.

9. Gently lay one Tyvek square over the hole, covering it totally.

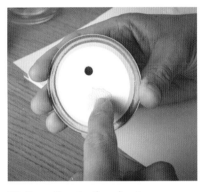

10. Press it onto the glue to secure.

11. Turn the lid over and glue around the SAME hole.

12. Push the second piece of Tyvek onto the glue over the same hole.

Continues →

13. Glue around the top side of the second hole and press the silicon injection port into it.

14. Ensure that the top of the port is on the top side of the lid!

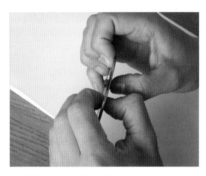

15. Make sure that the injection port pops through completely. It should fit tight.

16. Glue the seam on the underside of the injection port. Don't leave gaps.

17. It should look like this. This lid is all safe and is looking great.

18. When the glue is dried, it's ready to put on your jar and use.

Making Your Liquid Culture

Whether you want to use honey, other syrups or powdered sugars like light malt extract, 4% is a good concentration. That means 4 g of sugar topped up to 100 g with water. Technically, syrup is a mix of sugar and water, so 4 g of syrup contains less sugar than sugar in powder form; while we may be pedants, mushroom spores aren't, so they can cope just fine with small differences in sugar concentration. The whole process is incredibly simple. Just mix the correct amounts of honey and water, drop in the stir bar and secure the lid. We'll show you how to do that, though, because we're nice like that. Recipe for 16 oz liquid culture jar:

- 12 g honey
- 288 g water

Sterilizing Liquid Culture

Sterilization of liquid culture in Mason jars requires the same process as sterilizing grain jars or anything else, except that special care needs to be taken to ensure that the honey in the liquid culture does not caramelize. If the honey caramelizes then it can slow, or even stop the growth of spores. Sugars caramelize when exposed to high temperatures for too long, as a result of a reaction between the amino acids and sugars in a solution known as the Maillard reaction. As these compounds react, they become more complex, and complex sugars take more energy to break down into simple sugars, which can be used for mycelial growth. If it takes more energy to break down the caramelized sugar than the amount gained from its breakdown, that's a net energy loss for the mycelium—i.e., no growth. If the honey in your liquid culture has caramelized, it will be an amber color once it has been sterilized.

In most cases the honey in this recipe won't caramelize. At 15 psi / 250°F (121°C), 15 minutes should be enough to sterilize without drifting into caramelization. You may notice a few bits floating in your honey after taking it out of your pressure cooker. This is completely normal and the result of natural proteins and other compounds sticking together after heating. If you are worried you may have caramelized your liquid culture, this shouldn't be too much of a problem. Just inject a small volume of spores (see Inoculating Your Liquid Culture Medium later on) and see if it grows. However, in cases where you don't have much spore suspension left, it might be easier and less risky to just make a new batch of liquid culture—and this time pay attention to your timer!

133

Making the Liquid Culture Medium

1. Normal store-bought honey is fine for this process. No need for organic.

2. Weigh out 12 grams of honey in your Mason jar.

3. Add in 288g of water. Normal tap water works perfectly.

4. Drop in your stir bar. This will allow you to stir the culture without opening the jar.

5. Fasten the lid. Your jar is now ready for sterilization.

Sterilizing Liquid Culture Jars

1. Place the liquid culture jar into your pressure cooker. Add a quart of water.

2. The jar should sit on a trivet. If it's in the water, that's okay.

3. The trivet keeps the jar off the bottom of the pressure cooker for safety.

4. Securely close the pressure cooker and heat until it begins to hiss.

5. The weight will spin or rock. Keep the cooker at this stage for 10 minutes.

6. Turn off the heat and allow the pressure cooker to cool completely before opening.

Inoculating Your Liquid Culture Medium

It's especially important to consider sterility at this point, as you want to keep your liquid culture for a while and allowing in contaminants at this stage of the process will ruin any subsequent crop. Maintain your good working methods as outlined in the previous chapters and work as quickly as you can. You should be working inside your glove box throughout this process and be sure that you've adequately cleaned the inside with the 10% bleach solution before you start.

The method of inoculation for liquid culture jars is much the same as for PF Tek jars, grain jars or anything else.

For inoculating your liquid culture with a spore syringe, you need only 1-2 ml of suspension. Once the spores germinate, they'll multiply exponentially in the liquid.

For inoculating PF or grain jars, 1-2 ml of liquid culture will also be enough. It's important to make sure your needle is long enough and of a large enough gauge (diameter) so as not to get blocked with mycelium. We've used 19-21 gauge syringes (0.042-0.032 inches / 1.07-0.82 mm) without too much difficulty, but this should be seen as the lowest limit on the syringe gauge; any narrower and you might struggle to successfully collect any culture. It's also worth noting that larger diameters equal a smaller gauge number, so if you're shopping for needles on gauge value alone, you want lower than 21. Anywhere between 14 and 21 should be fine, and in terms of length, 1 and a half inches (40 mm) is great.

As the culture grows and feeds on the honey, the liquid will become clearer.

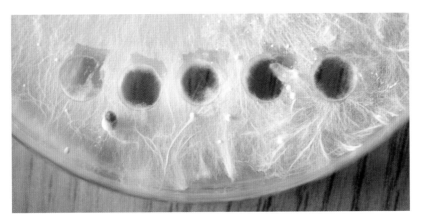

This agar plate, though already used, can be used to colonize a liquid culture.

Inoculating with Agar

Later in this book we'll show you how to work with agar (see Chapter 10). We love agar; it's fun, it's a great way to ensure sterility and it looks impressively professional. You can also use colonized agar to inoculate your liquid culture, which can work just as well as any other spore suspension.

The thing that stops most people from using this method is that to chop up large bits of colonized agar requires something that's big enough to do the job and can also be sterilized, either in a lab-grade autoclave or a fairly massive pressure cooker. This usually takes the form of a special type of blender, often made of stainless steel, as this can withstand the high temperatures needed to sterilize it. The problem with these is that they're not exactly easy to purchase and they cost up to $1,000. Not really suitable in any way for a home mushroom grow.

However, it isn't necessary to use a huge amount of agar in order to colonize a liquid medium. In theory (and, as we've found, in practice), all that's needed to colonize the liquid is a small amount of mycelium. By simply using a sterile scalpel, you can cut away a small amount of the agar and introduce this into the liquid culture inside of a glove box or flow hood. You can even make things easier by using a sterile syringe and stabbing the colonized agar a number of times, then injecting this straight into the liquid culture jar. This does mean that colonization won't take place as rapidly as if you had one of the expensive blenders and could inoculate with a larger amount of blended agar, but it will still work.

These "clouds" are the growing cultures. This liquid culture is healthy.

After Inoculation

Your inoculated culture should be placed into a warm, dark space to colonize. We recommend airing cupboards, wardrobes, anything that has high shelves and can be kept closed and clean. By placing any cultures high up, you're avoiding the plethora of floor-level contaminants that get stirred up any time someone walks by. You can use your stir plate to stir the liquid culture as much as you see fit, although once a day, after you see little clumps of mycelium forming, is a pretty good benchmark. This will distribute the culture around the medium and encourage faster and more widespread growth.

After inoculation, the mushroom cultures will feed on the sugars in the solution, creating little clusters that will be suspended in the liquid. These will then grow and expand. In the few days after inoculation, you'll start to see little clouds of culture forming in the center of the jar. These will become thicker and more opaque as the colonization progresses. When your liquid culture is fully colonized, the liquid part of the culture will be almost perfectly clear. This should take about two weeks to a month. After a good amount of culture has developed, you can slow down mycelial

Cover your liquid culture with foil to protect the filter during cold storage.

growth by placing your liquid culture jar into the fridge, in a place where it's not likely to be knocked over or disturbed too much. The top shelf of the fridge is a good place to store your liquid culture, as there's nothing above it to drip down and potentially soak your air filter and introduce contaminants. However, if you have to put your liquid culture elsewhere in the fridge, contamination problems can be prevented by covering your jar lid with a square of kitchen foil.

It is possible to make larger amounts of liquid culture using the method we've outlined. When you get to quarts, you'll need to scale the amounts of water, honey and spore suspension properly to ensure that the process will work, but apart from that, expanding this method is quite simple. If you did want to start making amounts above a quart, you will need to source some slightly more professional equipment such as a flow hood or a larger glove box. However, for the regular home grower, the amount we've shown here should be ample and should last for a long while. We've had liquid culture jars that have lasted us for at least a year and have stayed viable the whole time. Follow basic sterilization methods every time you use it and you should enjoy great results from it for months.

These shrooms have been properly dried, so they won't succumb to mold.

Potential Problems

As with anything in this book, a non-sterile working environment can allow for contamination of the growing medium and fuck up the whole shebang. Contamination of liquid cultures can be especially difficult to diagnose, as fuzzy clumps of green mold, which appear white in their early stages, look very similar to mushroom mycelium. While agar work (see Chapter 10) can help identify potential contaminants, this also requires a sterile environment. New airborne contaminants can get mixed up in the liquid culture transfer process, potentially giving you a false indication of contamination. Often the only way to identify contaminants in your liquid culture is to inoculate a small test batch (a single PF jar, or 100 g of grain), cross your fingers and hope for that nice white color and mushroomy smell.

For this reason, you should be especially cognizant of your environment while using the methods mentioned. Unless you're confident in your sterile technique and / or have access to a flow hood, we recommend using only high-quality inoculum for your liquid culture. This includes quality vendor-produced spore syringes or flow-hood prepared samples and agar isolates. As liquid culture should form the basis of your culture line, getting it right

This liquid culture has become contaminated and should be disposed of.

the first time is essential. A well-colonized, clean liquid culture will resist further contamination, so repeated use of a quality culture shouldn't cause you too many problems.

Sometimes, you might find that your liquid culture fails to grow after inoculation. This can be for a number of reasons. If you've used a small amount of the spores, it might be that growth won't show until a week or even two weeks later. In this case, just sit tight and see what happens.

Sometimes, you can find that your "clouds" of cultures have darker specks or spots in them. This looks a lot like the start of mold and can be quite worrying. Don't freak out; if your cultures are growing well and rapidly, it might be that they are simply spore clumps; bits of dead spores that failed to germinate, or simply densely collected germinated spores. It could also be that the mycelium is growing around clumps of proteins or other compounds that had formed during the heating process. If you do see these, don't instantly assume contamination, as we've found this is quite common with honey. Keep an eye on your liquid culture, and if the spots don't grow, the culture is most likely fine. However, if these darker spots do start to grow and your culture takes on an odd-colored hue, you should throw away the jar and start again.

Grain

Once you have got the hang of the PF Tek, you might find yourself wanting to try growing from grain. Whilst you can grow mushrooms directly from grain jars, the main aim of grain is to rapidly increase your production through grain-to-grain transfer and spawning to bulk substrates (see Chapter 9).

There are many types of different grain, and nearly all types are suitable for growing magic mushroom spawn. Rye has established itself as the classic choice for most home growers, but wild birdseed mix and popcorn are also commonly used. Commercial growers sometimes mix their grain, in an art-meets-science attempt to maximize production. In reality, any whole grain will work, it's just a personal choice often decided by ease of preparation, cost or local availability. We'll show you how to use rye grain, birdseed and popcorn in this chapter, as they're the most widely available and are ones that we've had the most success with.

No matter what type of grain you use, it cannot be utilized without some amount of preparation. The grain needs to be rendered in a way that the mycelium can extract nutrients from it. There are, in general, two main ways to prepare your grain.

The first method involves mixing dry grain with the desired amount of

Working with grain allows you to scale up to bulk substrates like manure.

Grain jars are an excellent way to scale up a relatively basic grow.

Here you can see excellent rhizomorphic growth on rye grain.

This popcorn is becoming colonized by the colonized rye grain.

water in the spawn containers and leaving it to hydrate overnight. These containers are then shaken to redistribute the moisture content, then autoclaved (pressure-cooked).

The second is to soak the grain in water, usually overnight, bring the whole mixture to a boil, then drain off excess moisture. The grain is then packaged into spawn containers before autoclaving as in the first method.

People will often argue about which method is most suitable, citing factors such as moisture distribution or cleanliness. Ultimately we think both methods are suitable, though one method may be preferred depending on the amount or type of grain you're working with. In this chapter we'll show you how to do the first method with rye, and the second method with popcorn and wild birdseed.

A Word on Moisture Capacity

It's worth noting that different grains have different moisture capacities when fully hydrated. This is the amount of water that can be held within a given grain type. As you reduce your grain volume, the proportion of water should increase. With increasing grain volume comes an increasing chance of the center of the grain mass becoming oxygen-deprived (anaerobic core). This in turn creates an unfavorable environment for mycelium, which

145

a reduced moisture content and increased sterilization time seeks to remedy at larger grain masses. A handy table of how to adjust your moisture, sterilization time and gypsum addition, depending on your initial amount of rye, can be found in the Rye Scaling section below. We've provided some rough moisture capacity calculations for 1 kg of rye, wild birdseed and popcorn to get you started, but moisture capacity can vary depending on things like ambient humidity, age of grain and supplier.

Grain type	⊜ Rye	◔ Popcorn	⬭ Wild birdseed
Dry mass	1 kg	1 kg	1 kg
Hydrated mass	1.75 kg	1.6 kg	1.4 kg
Moisture capacity	43%	37.5%	28.5%

Although this has little effect on suitability as a substrate, if you're trying to calculate easy water-to-grain ratios for using the second method (see above), you might like to do some tests of moisture content. Weigh out a small amount of your unhydrated grain (around 100 g), then dry in an oven overnight (around eight hours) at 300°F (149°C). After this, reweigh your grain; this will tell you the true dry mass. Soak your grain for 12–24 hours, then simmer on a low heat for 15 minutes to an hour. Drain well and allow to cool, then finally measure one more time. This will give you the fully hydrated mass of your 100 g sample. With these two values, you can easily calculate moisture capacity using the following formula:

$$\text{moisture capacity (\%)} = \frac{\text{hydrated mass} - \text{dry mass}}{\text{hydrated mass}} \times 100$$

If you're not producing a lot of grain on a regular basis or looking to make your own grain formulas, such a calculation may be overcomplicated and unnecessary. By following our methods below we can guarantee you'll have perfectly prepared grain every time!

Grain Containers

To work with grain, you'll need something to hold that grain. We use both one-quart Mason jars and pre-sterilized spawn bags for this. Spawn bags are capable of withstanding the high temperatures necessary to properly sterilize the contents while still being malleable enough to work with. They also should have a filtered micro-porous vent to allow for airflow into and out of the bags. You can buy these from any online mush-room-growing vendor; they're used by growers of edible mushrooms, too, and they're usually less than a dollar per bag. To use these grain bags properly, you'll need an im-pulse sealer to close them after the grain has been put inside but be-fore sterilization. If you're moving into intermediate mushroom-grow-ing techniques, then an impulse sealer is a worthwhile investment. You can get them for about $20 at the usual online retail stores.

We use one-quart jars for grain work. These are the perfect size.

It's worth having autoclave tape on hand as well, to ensure that your bag is properly sterile once you've pressure-cooked it with the grain inside. Autoclave tape has lines that turn black once an adequate temperature has been reached for an adequate time to ensure sterilization. The lines stay black, allowing you to see easily which bags you've sterilized and which you haven't. It's worth noting that although the tape will tell you that the correct temperature has been reached, it won't tell you how long it's been there for. Keep an eye on the time and make sure you're not rushing jars through the sterilization step.

We actually created our own injectable grain bag by placing a blob of silicon sealant onto the outside of a spawn bag and letting it dry. This forms a self-healing inoculation port through which to inject liquid culture. Spore syringes aren't really suitable for grain bags as the bags contain larger amounts of substrate and therefore take longer to colonize.

If you choose to use jars, you'll be working with slightly less grain per container, but this isn't a real problem; you can always have more jars! You will, however, need to create lids that allow for air exchange; we'll show you how to do this.

Rhizomorphic growth spreads along the bottom of a grain jar.

Grain Jars

We'll show you how to make one-quart rye grain jars using the in-jar soak method mentioned earlier. These are a great starting point for those looking to get into grain. Obviously, you'll need jars of a suitable size to do this, but you'll also need to modify the canning lids to ensure that air can flow into and out of your jars to allow the grain to breathe. There are two types of lids you can make here.

Lid Types

1. Full Tyvek. This is where you drill three or four holes in your jar lids, then screw a layer of Tyvek between the lid and the screw band. By keeping the lid on the inside, it prevents the grain from wetting the Tyvek. If the Tyvek is wet, contaminants can grow through the lid from the outside and into your precious spawn. These are better for grain-to-grain transfer, under a flow hood, as assembling them can be tricky.

Self-healing injection ports. Mark with a marker once used.

2. Self-healing injection ports. You can buy silicon injection ports from the usual online retailers. These allow you to inject liquid culture or spores directly into your grain quickly and easily, without any mess. Just drill an appropriate-sized hole in your lid and push the silicon port through. It's best if you drill the hole a little tight, so that it holds the injection port in place. If you drill it too big, or are just super methodical like us, you can add a little heat resistant adhesive to seal up the gaps. Finally, drill one more one-eighth-inch hole and glue a small piece of Tyvek on both sides for air exchange.

3. Pillow stuffing filters. By drilling a larger hole (three-quarter-inch) in your lids and stuffing them with a small wad of polyester pillow stuffing, you have an injection site and filter all in one. We avoid this method as the idea of getting grain tangled in the stuffing seems like too much

Lids with larger ventilation ports are perfect for grain jars.

mess, so we simply glue a big square of Tyvek on both sides. The downside is you can't inject through this, but we use the self-healing lids for this anyway. It's good to have a few lying around for grain-to-grain jars, as they're easy to make quickly and work just great.

No matter which method you choose, ensure that you have one lid per jar and that you've got enough jars to hold whatever amount of grain you've chosen to work with.

We use organic rye grain for this process, but non-organic is also fine.

Prepping Grain Jars

1. Weigh out 220 g of rye grain and measure 200 ml of water. Tap water is fine.

2. Add the grain to the jar and mark the level with a permanent marker.

3. Add in the water, being careful not to spill.

4. Gently swirl the jar to mix the water and the rye grain together.

5. With a permanent pen, mark the level of the water. Set the lid on the jar.

Soaking Your Grain

We're going to use the soaking method with our rye grain here, to show you how it's done. As mentioned above, this involves pouring both grain and water into your jars, leaving them to soak, then sterilizing them in your pressure cooker to ensure that no contaminants remain. This is an incredibly simple method as long as your sterilization procedure is done properly, and you correctly weigh out both the grain and the water.

For a one-quart grain jar, you'll need:

- 220 g rye grain
- 200 ml water
- 1 g gypsum (around a teaspoon is fine)

Scaling Grain

If you're working with bags, you will probably want to use more grain. We've included some handy charts that let you figure out how much water and gypsum to add to any given amount of dried grain up to 3.3 kg. However, we've also included a chart for sterilization times; it will be this aspect that limits the home grower. As bags get more full, longer time is required for the steam to penetrate the center of the mass of grain and raise the temperature to achieve suitable sterilization. Most home pressure cookers can't hold high volumes of grain; if your bags are touching the sides they may melt or burn your grain. In addition, longer sterilization times increase the risk of you boiling your pressure cooker dry, which is bad for both your pressure cooker and your grain, as both can burn.

Sterilization

Once your grain jars have been set aside for 24 hours, it's time to sterilize them. For this, we're going to use the pressure cooker method outlined in Chapter 6. Remember not to let the bottom of your jars touch the bottom of the pressure cooker or you risk burning the grain. Jars should be above the water level and will most likely be laid on their sides so that they fit into the pressure cooker. If this is the case, we like to sit a spare canning lid under the lid end of the jar, to lift that end up slightly and ensure that no water will leak out or splash up onto the Tyvek airflow port.

You might smell the grain when you're sterilizing it, leading you to believe that it's actually cooking. This is okay, and totally normal. However,

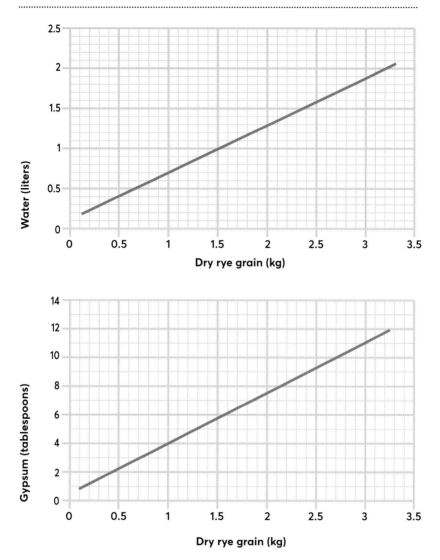

Amounts of water, gypsum and sterilization time for scaled up grain.

if the grain smells like it's burning, you should check the pressure cooker. It may need more water, or the bag / jar may be touching the bottom of the cooker. This shouldn't be the case; there should always be a shelf to prevent the bottom of the container from sitting on the bottom of the cooker. Fix the issue and start again. However, if you have burned your grain a little, don't despair. If the damage isn't too bad, you can disperse

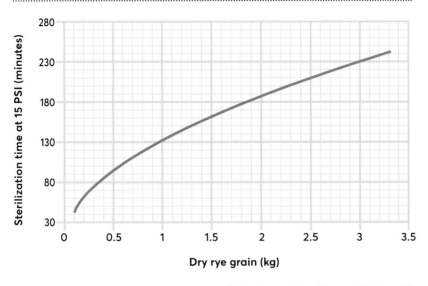

the burned grains throughout the rest of the jar and it will most likely still work. We've done this before and the colonization of the jar has still been successful. However, if your whole jar is black, and your kitchen smells like burnt caramel, it's probably a good sign to try again!

After sterilization, allow your jars to cool until they're cold to the touch. Once they're cool, they're ready to be inoculated immediately.

Inoculation

Now that your grain is fully sterile, you need to introduce a culture to your jar. This can be done using a spore syringe or by using already colonized grain in a grain-to-grain transfer. For more information on this, read on. Here, we'll show you how to inoculate from a liquid culture syringe.

The inoculation method here is basically the same as the one used in PF Tek, in principle at least. The main difference is that you will be inoculating through either your self-healing injection port or directly through your filter in the case of Poly-Fil lids. As we mentioned earlier, full Tyvek lids aren't really suitable for syringe inoculation; it's best to save these for grain-to-grain transfers.

Grain Bags

If you'd like to work with larger amounts of substrate, then grain bags are a fantastic way to do this. Bags come in various shapes and sizes, but it's important to choose ones from a dedicated mushroom-grow supplier as their bags are designed with all your requirements in mind. Keep a lookout for 0.2 micron air filters, as they allow air exchange while filtering out all contaminants. Some growers may tell you how they can get away with 0.5 microns, however *P. cubensis* is less contamination-resistant than other mushroom species (e.g., oysters) and we recommend staying away from these. We use Unicorn's Type 3T Bag and we love them.

Some bags have self-healing injection ports on them, which is a great way to inoculate with liquid culture, as you would with jars. When working with liquid culture, we prefer jars as they're easier to handle and can be re-cycled—saving the world from yet more plastic waste.

If you like the method above, wherein you soak the grain in its container then sterilize the whole thing, it's very easy to use this same process with bags instead of jars. Grain bags are (or at least should be—always double check!) autoclavable, which means that they can stand up to the high temperatures necessary to sterilize the bag's contents. The process is much the same as above,

These grain jars have been shaken, dispersing the mycelium throughout the uncolonized grain.

Grain jars that aren't properly sterilized may become contaminated with mold, like this one.

but we explain how to do it with grain bags, because we're nice like that.

Next we're going to show you how to use the soak and boil method with birdseed and popcorn, although you can use the pressure cooker method outlined above with birdseed and popcorn, too; just be aware that there are differences in moisture capacity between these grains, so experiment with different volumes. It doesn't matter whether you use popcorn in jars, rye grain in bags, birdseed in bags; these methods and containers are all interchangeable. It's just a matter of preference.

Preparing Your Popcorn / Birdseed

With this method, the grain is soaked and then boiled before being placed into the spawn bags. When using this method, bear in mind that birdseed will expand about 25% after soaking, so you'll need to allow for this in the water container you soak it in.

When you pour water into a bowl of birdseed, you'll see that the black

Inoculating Grain Jars

1. To sterilize your glove box, measure out one part bleach.

2. Add nine parts water to the bleach. Clean the inside of your glove box with this solution.

3. Sterilize your needle by heating it with a lighter. Keep it red for several seconds.

4. Wipe the top and sides of your grain jars with the bleach solution.

5. Push your liquid culture–loaded syringe gently into the middle of the injection port.

6. When the needle is inside the jar, slowly push the syringe to inject the liquid culture.

7. Pull out the needle slowly. The injection port will be slightly stained; this is fine.

8. Wipe the top of the grain jar with the bleach solution again. Repeat with the other jars.

Inoculation should always be done inside a sterilized glove box.

Use your 10% bleach solution to wipe down the jars before inoculation.

sunflower seeds rise to the top of the water. Some growers remove these, some leave them in; it's a matter of personal preference. We scoop ours out, as it's easy to do and it helps to create a more homogenous grain size for even colonization. Leave them in if you want; we welcome rule breaking. You shouldn't soak birdseed for more than 12 hours, as fermentation may begin to occur if you leave it too long. Drain in a large colander.

Boiling

When your grain has been soaked and drained properly, it's time to boil it. Drain the water from it and transfer it to a large pot, then add fresh water. The water line should be a couple of inches above the grain. Bring to a boil and then take the heat down to allow for a simmer. Simmer the grain for 45 to 60 minutes, stirring often to make sure that no grains are burning to the bottom of the pan. With popcorn, some of your kernels will burst a little; this is okay, but you ideally don't want this to happen. Keep an eye on your grains.

After an hour, remove your pot from the heat and drain the grain in a colander. It's incredibly important to drain these grains well after soaking; you should leave them for 30 minutes or more, until there are absolutely no droplets coming from the strainer or colander.

Inside a glove box, you can lift the lid of a grain jar to inoculate with liquid culture.

Soaking Grain in Your Grain Bags

1. Weigh out 240 g of your rye grain. Make sure this is accurate.

2. Add the rye grain into the bag, making sure not to lose any!

3. Drop the bag on the counter a few times to settle the grain.

4. Add in 185 ml of water. Tap water is fine for this.

5. It'll look a little weird, like this, but that's totally normal.

6. Loosely fold down the top of the bag. We want airflow to be possible.

7. This filter patch keeps contaminants out and lets air in.

8. Leave the bag to soak overnight. The next morning, it'll look like this.

9. Fold the bag and loosely tape closed with autoclave tape.

10. Sterilize as instructed on page 163.

Soaking Bird Seed for Grain Bags

1. You'll need 1 kg bag of birdseed, a sieve, a large bowl and some water.

2. Empty the birdseed into the bowl. All of it!

3. Fill up the bowl with water until the birdseed is totally submerged.

4. The black sunflower seeds in the mixture will float to the top.

5. Using the sieve, remove the black sunflower seeds and dispose of them.

6. Allow the birdseed to soak overnight or for 12 hours.

Sterilization

Fill your bags as much as you'd like, but bear in mind the limitations that we mentioned earlier in terms of sterilization time and the capacity of your pressure cooker (see the section on Scaling Grain above).

Keep in mind that the bags will swell during sterilization due to changes in pressure inside your pressure cooker. This means that you don't want to seal your bags too tightly as changes in pressure can cause them to pop. The bags need to be sealed in a way that allows air in and out, but without being completely open (as this will leave them exposed to contamina-

Some boiled corn kernels will pop. This is totally fine; they can be used.

tion as soon as you open your pressure cooker). We like to roll down the bags to remove any excess air and loosely seal them with a wooden clothespin (plastic will melt) or some autoclave tape. These will most likely pop open, but don't worry; as long as your bags haven't unrolled completely you'll be okay.

When your bags are ready, use the same pressure-cooker method as previously described. Ensure again that the bags aren't touching the bottom or sides of the pressure cooker; most cookers come with a trivet to raise things up slightly, so be sure to use that. As with the rye grain, there may be a slight cooking smell, but this is okay.

Inoculation

For the first-time home grower, inoculating bags can be tricky. As you move towards large volumes of grain, the amount of spawn you can generate increases greatly but so do risks of contamination as a result of the scaling issues we mentioned earlier. We're slightly biased towards jars, due to the limitations of our home set up and the fact that throwing away a jar or two of contaminated grain doesn't prove to be as much of a setback as tossing a kilo or two in a bag.

We've had far more contamination problems with bags and zero (so far) with jars. As a result, we recommend you only use bags for grain-to-grain as it reduces the colonization time and chance of contamination.

Loading Your Grain Bags With Presoaked Grain

1. Ensure that your birdseed or popcorn has been well drained.

2. Fill the grain bag with the drained birdseed or popcorn.

3. Your bag shouldn't be much fuller than this. They can be too full.

4. Drop the bag on the counter a few times to settle the grain.

5. Grab the grain bag just above the grain level. Remove excess air.

6. Fold the rest of the grain bag so it's tucked away neatly.

7. Now it's ready to be secured with autoclave tape and sterilized!

It's best to perform transfers when your grain jars have just become fully colonized, like this one.

Here you can see how the mycelium overwhelms the grain medium.

Grain-to-Grain Transfer

This is one of the best and most successful ways to turn a small amount of colonized grain into a large amount of colonized grain. It will save you time and effort, and it will help you to easily expand your grow without spending much more money. The method uses an already colonized substrate, meaning that you won't need to use any more of your liquid culture or purchase a new spore syringe. It will also cut down on time, as the spores are already germinated and will be eager to colonize the new medium. In fact, as soon as you transfer the colonized grain into the new jar, the growth will be explosive—which is always great to see. If you use a one-quart jar of colonized grain to inoculate four one-quart jars of un-colonized grain, the new jars should be fully colonized in about seven days.

The theory behind grain-to-grain transfer is simple: once you have a sterile, colonized grain jar, you simply pour some of this colonized grain into an un-colonized, freshly sterilized grain jar, and allow the mycelium to grow onto the new grain and colonize the new jar in total. The transfer itself is incredibly simple and will work every time as long as your grain is sterile and you perform the transfer inside a glove box. That being said, it's a good idea to thoroughly check your jars for any obvious signs of contamination. Later jars can easily be thrown out, but early contamination can ruin a whole batch. Molds like *Trichoderma* and *Penicillium* can grow much quicker than mushroom mycelium, so even the slightest

165

Grain-to-grain transfers should take place in a flow hood or glove box, like this.

sign of contamination isn't worth risking.

It's best to use your grain jars when they've just become fully colonized. At this point, the mycelium is just coming to the end of exponential growth so it will quickly spread through any new substrate. You can let them sit for a week or two, but if you do face a situation where you can't use the colonized grain for a while, it's best to put it into the fridge to slow down the process. Leave any jar for too long and it will start pinning in vitro— i.e., growing mushrooms while still in the jar.

We use one one-quart jar of colonized grain to inoculate four one-quart jars of un-colonized grain. The resulting growth is rapid and vigorous, and we like this. You could use one one-quart jar of colonized grain to colonize up to 40 one-quart jars of un-colonized grain if you so wished, but this method is normally used only by commercial edible-growers looking to maximize their spawn productivity and runs the risk of high contamination for a home hobby-grower like yourself. The decisions on what spawn ratio to use varies from grower to grower, and

Grain jars receiving a grain-to-grain transfer do not need lids with injection ports.

Grain-to-grain Transfer

1. Grab your colonized grain jar and however many uncolonized jars you wish to inoculate.

2. The best way to break up colonized grain is to hit the jar against a bike tire.

3. As the lump of colonized grain breaks up it will appear to turn less white.

4. Keep going until there are no lumps of grain left.

5. Make sure you know which jar is colonized and which aren't! *Continues →*

6. Loosen the lids on both / all your jars but don't remove.

7. Only lift the lid off the jar when ready to perform the transfer.

8. Quickly lift the lid off the receiving jar and pour the correct amount of colonized grain into it.

9. Replace the lids immediately. Do not leave the jars open longer than necessary.

10. Secure the lids fully after the transfer has been completed.

it's normally driven by factors such as time, sterility, substrate availability and desired yield. Feel free to experiment and find out what suits your needs.

You don't have to use all your colonized grain at once; you can use any amount that you need and save the rest. Simply place the lid back onto the colonized jar and keep it in the fridge until you need it. When you're ready to use it again,

> ### 🍄 Use a Glove Box
> We have performed this grain-to-grain transfer outside of the glove box to allow you to see exactly what's going on. However, this should ALWAYS be done inside a glove box, as the grain will be exposed to the open air and therefore should be in a sterile environment.

take it out of the fridge the night before to give the mycelium time to warm up before you transfer it.

Grain-to-Grain Transfer into Spawn Bags

You can also perform grain transfers into pre-sterilized spawn bags. This works in much the same way, except that you're likely to have a larger amount of uncolonized grain in the spawn bag, so make sure you adjust your transfer amount to account for this. This is another good way to make your culture go further.

After transferring to spawn bags, it's a good idea to use an impulse sealer to ensure the bag has an airtight seal. This makes it much easier to handle the bags at a later date when it comes to shaking the contents to encourage rapid colonization.

Transferring from Transfers

Once you've colonized the new jars and left them to incubate, they'll eventually grow and become entirely colonized. From here, you can break up the colonized grain and use it to spawn to bulk substrate such as manure, straw or coir. It's generally accepted that you should only perform grain-to-grain transfers with the same culture two times; over three generations, if you will. At a 1:10 transfer rate (a sensible upper limit for the home grower) a single parent jar will colonize 10 "children" jars, and each child jar will colonize another 10 "grandchildren" jars, giving you 100 times the initial volume of spawn across just two transfers! Whilst commercial edible growers can

Shaking up partially colonized grain bags will allow for quicker colonization.

When you start transferring from transfers, good labelling is essential.

After transferring to grain bags, an impulse sealer will help keep an airtight seal.

successfully generate fourth-generation spawn, most home growers neither need this amount nor have the level of contamination control to make this a viable option. With each new colonization, the culture's growth will be less vigorous and will have noticeably declined by the time you reach the great-grandchildren jars. Still, you've got a potential 100 jars of colonized grain out of one initial jar here, so don't be too disheartened!

Fruiting Grain Jars or Grain Bags Directly

When your grain jars or bags are fully colonized, the next step is to use the grain to inoculate a bulk substrate, such as horse manure. We'll show you how to do this in the next chapter. However, you can also allow the substrate to fruit directly inside the jars or bags, if you really prefer. This is the lazy method and won't allow much room for the fruit to grow, and you may also run into issues with airflow when relying on the small venting holes in your jar lids or bags. However, you can still get a fairly respectable crop of

Mycelium will grow down into the jar, as shown here.

This is some fantastic rhizomorphic growth, which is exactly what we want.

While you can grab the top mushrooms here, the ones underneath are trapped.

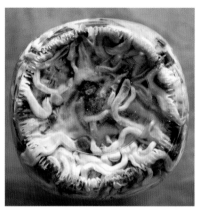

Mushrooms are tenacious and will grow wherever they can.

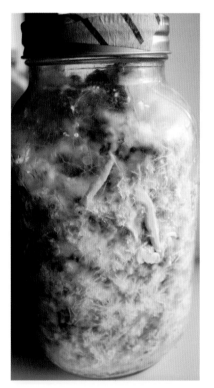

This jar has pinned in vitro and has been left to grow this way for a long while.

It will be next to impossible to get these mushrooms out of this jar!

If you leave your jars to pin in vitro the growth will be sparse and the mushrooms misshapen and—well, just plain weird. You can still consume them though.

mushrooms this way, and if you find that you have a colonized jar with no bulk substrate to inoculate, this may be your best choice. Just pop these into a terrarium or other fruiting chamber and let nature take its course.

If you leave your colonized jars too long for any reason, they will start pinning in vitro whether you like it or not. If this is your intention, you should place your jars into some natural light and ensure that they're not in a cold area. If it's too cold, they won't grow. Your mushrooms will grow slower and the yields will be much less than if they were in a terrarium, but the growth will still occur.

173

Bulk Substrate Method and Pasteurization

If you're looking to expand your grow in terms of size rather than complexity, you need to get down with some bulk substrates. The term refers to any sort of nutritious material that can be colonized in large amounts, usually with grain spawn, yielding a larger amount of mushrooms than you could achieve with other methods (though most people exclude sawdust when using this term). When paired with the methods you've learned for cultivating on grain in Chapter 8, this is an easy and incredibly affordable technique with a huge return on investment.

When your grain jars are fully colonized, you can take your prepared bulk substrate and simply mix the grain into the substrate in a clean environment.

The mycelium will be dying for some more nutritious material to reach out and cover, so by spreading the colonized grain throughout the bulk substrate, you'll encourage vigorous and expansive mycelial growth—and lots of mycelial growth results in lots of mushrooms. When your substrate is fully colonized, you'll induce pinning via light and a reduction in CO_2, and boom: mushrooms will pop up out of your substrate.

Just as with grains, there is a variety of bulk substrate recipes that can be used to produce a huge crop of mushrooms. Manure, straw and supplemented

Behold the glorious bounty of a monotub. Lighter for scale.

Bulk substrates yield larger mushrooms in greater numbers.

coir (supplements include used coffee grounds, worm castings, wheat bran and even cardboard) are all suitable bulk substrates. Everyone has their own favorite recipe and some will defend it to the grave, but as with grain, most sensible suggestions will work (in fact not just sensible ones; try Googling "oyster mushroom armchair" or "magic mushroom holy bible"). We like manure, as it's free if you know where to look, requires very little preparation and colonizes very evenly. In addition, having been preprocessed (it's essentially

176

These fully colonized grain jars can now inoculate a bulk substrate.

These grain jars still need a little while to reach full colonization.

These beauties are growing on a horse manure substrate.

digested straw / hay), it's loaded with beneficial microorganisms that help break down the more complex carbohydrates and proteins in the manure to more accessible simple sugars and amino acids for your mushrooms to thrive on. One of these is called Firefang (an ascomycete), so named for its ability to induce spontaneous combustion in improperly prepared compost—and that's just badass. However, it's rare and requires large volumes of compacted hay, so don't worry about your little grow catching fire.

They're oddly shaped at first, but as they get bigger, they'll even out.

Manure

Psilocybe cubensis is a coprophilous species, meaning that it just *loves* poo. The poo of certain animals provides a nitrogen-rich environment for the mushrooms, and in nature, the digestive enzymes in the stomach of the animal help break down complex nutrients, allowing the mushrooms to grow rapidly. There are a couple of different types of manure that *P. cubensis* will grow on; cow and horse shit particularly. If you're lucky enough to live on or near a farm, you'll most likely have an accessible and constant source of both of these. However, for those of you who don't live at the back end of nowhere, you'll most likely be growing on horse manure. This is great, as horse manure has a better consistency than cow manure, which requires

178

What a looker! This will grow into a sizeable specimen.

A manure monotub in its third flush—and it won't be the last!

Shrooms love manure. Here are some babies growing on manure in the wild!

more supplements to compensate for its naturally higher moisture content.

It's incredibly important to get very dry, field-aged manure for this process, as fresh manure contains too much ammonia and other nutrients, which will not only stink out your house, but also encourage contamination. For most people, it's much easier to find horse poo that meets these requirements; horse shit dries more evenly and is more likely to stay together enough to be field-aged, whereas cow shit is, if you'll pardon the phrase, a hot mess.

If all you can find is fresh horse manure (we've all been there), you can dry it out pretty easily by leaving it where it is and letting nature take its course. If you really can't leave it, or are worried a competing grower might come and swipe your stash, take it home and lay it out in the sun on a tarp in the garden. When it's ready, it will break apart easily and be devoid of almost any smell.

Horse poop provides a nitrogen-rich environment for P. cubensis.

You can also grow on elephant manure, if you happen to have it lying around. However, if you live in a place where elephants are dropping turds on your doorstep we suggest you concentrate on remedying that situation rather than growing

180

You need field-aged manure, on the left. The poop on the right is too fresh.

This is perfectly field-aged for our purposes.

Break open the manure balls; if it's field-aged, it should have absolutely no smell and be near-crunchy.

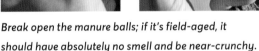

massive amounts of mushrooms. Alternatively, perhaps you've taken massive amounts of mushrooms and that's why you're seeing the elephants in the first place.

If you don't fancy wandering around the nearest fields searching for poo that's not too fresh, then most garden centers will sell some form of manure that's ready for horticultural use—and since many gardeners and non-psilocybin cultivators use this as a substrate or additive, you don't need to worry about appearing sketchy.

For this chapter, we'll be using horse manure, but these methods apply to any manure. As long as the animal eats grain or grass, mushrooms should grow on its shit. If donkeys, deer or moose are local to your area, then take yourself out poo-hunting and grow some awesome mushrooms.

If all you can find is fresh manure, you can dry it on a tarp in your garden.

Breaking Up Your Manure

The manure you've collected will most likely be formed into flat, roughly shaped discs or lumps, as it will have been trodden on and kicked about while it dried out. To use it as a substrate, you need to ensure that the manure is broken down into smaller pieces to allow the mycelium to grow through and around it.

When your shit is dry enough, put on some heavy gardening gloves and set to work crumbling it between your thumbs and forefingers, using the same method as you would to create a crumble topping from flour, butter and sugar. Rub the manure between your hands until it breaks up, allowing it to fall into a container (not on the floor). Make sure there are no larger pieces present in the mix when you're done, then your poo is ready to go.

Collect a ton of poop. Not a literal ton ... but lots.

Additives

You can use "straight" horse manure without any ill effects, but we always like to cut our shit with something

Breaking Up Your Manure

1. Ensure that all your manure is properly field-aged. It should look like this.

2. Make sure you have enough to almost fill your monotub.

3. Strap on your thick gardening gloves for safety reasons.

4. Break up the manure by crumbling it between your thumbs and forefingers.

5. Rub the manure until it breaks up and falls into a container.

6. When manure is like this, mycelium can grow through and into it.

183

These PF Tek mushrooms aren't huge, but they're potent.

to encourage aeration, as this aids in rhizomorphic growth and stops the substrate from becoming too wet. Mushrooms are decomposers, meaning that they'll break down just about anything organic, but there are a number of additives that are said to add particular benefits to the substrate.

Vermiculite

We add 20% vermiculite by volume to our horse manure, and that's about it. The vermiculite will allow you to add a bit more moisture without making the mixture too "muddy" and will bring some texture into the manure. Some growers would add one part vermiculite to one part horse manure, but we don't feel that this is entirely necessary (and why waste perfectly good vermiculite when you don't have to?).

Coffee

It's not hard to get your hands on used coffee grounds. Even if you're not a slave to the caffeine as so many of us are, your local coffee shop will most likely provide you with an unending supply of their used grounds, and this means that you'll have plenty to mix in with your horse manure. Coffee grounds are said to release nitrogen as they degrade, and contain magnesium, phosphorous and potassium as well. Some mushroom cultivators use coffee grounds at 30% by volume and report great results.

Worm Castings

Also known as vermicast or vermicompost, this is an organic fertilizer produced by earthworms. After the worms have broken down organic matter, this is what remains, and it has a high saturation of nutrients as well as a low level of contaminants, making it perfect for use in a substrate. Worm castings also help your manure to hold moisture better, and therefore help your mushrooms to grow more vigorously. Add between 5 and 15% by volume.

Coir

Coconut coir is a material made from the fibrous inner shell of a coconut, known as the husk. Coir doesn't have a high nutrient content, but it helps aerate the substrate and breaks it up, resulting in a looser substrate with more room for the mycelium to stretch and grow. It's easy to work with and comes dry, making it popular with a whole host of horticulturists as it makes it easy to accurately assess the moisture content of your substrate even when coir is added.

Gypsum

Gypsum (a.k.a. calcium sulfate) is a great mineral additive and is useful in a variety of growing stages. Its main advantage is that it provides a great source of calcium and sulphur for mushroom growth. In addition, it improves bulk substrate aeration, improves moisture retention, avoids over wetting, prevents clumping and counteracts potentially harmful elements such as magnesium and sodium. No bulk grow should be without it and we use it at 5% by volume in our horse manure substrate.

When adding nutritional supplements, it's worth noting that you can have too much of a good thing. In theory, the more nutrients you introduce into your substrate, the more will be available for mushroom growth. However, with increased nutrition comes increased contamination risk. This is why some growers say that some substrates are too nutritious; coffee is a good example of this. If you must supplement, do it sparingly, keep good notes on contamination events and yield and decide if it's worth the extra risk for a few more mushrooms.

Making Powdered Gypsum

1. Grab some drywall chunks. We pulled ours out of a dumpster.

2. Drywall is almost pure gypsum, which is calcium sulfate.

3. Break it up into chunks small enough to fit in your blender or grinder.

4. You'll need to do this in small portions. Don't overfill the grinder.

5. Turn the drywall chunks to powder by pulsing in a grinder.

6. Sift the powdered gypsum to get rid of the paper.

7. Repeat this process until you've powdered all the drywall.

8. This should be leftover in the sieve. Bin it.

9. The resulting gypsum powder should look like this. Perfect!

Mixing Your Manure Substrate

1. Your manure should be completely dry and well broken up like this.

2. We add 20% vermiculite by volume.

3. Use a large container for this. You'll need the space for mixing.

4. Make sure you're using dry vermiculite for this process.

Field Capacity

With both bulk substrate and casing, you will need to add a suitable amount of water to optimize mycelial growth. Due to the variety of recipes and additives growers use, it's difficult to suggest a standard volume or proportion of water to add. As a result, a far more esoteric, but effective, standard is used; that of field capacity. In practice, field capacity is defined using three simple tests, beginning with a handful of your hydrated substrate:

1. Loosely held, there should be no dripping liquid coming from your hand.
2. Apply a gentle squeeze; a few drops should fall.

5. Dump the vermiculite in with the manure.

6. One part gypsum is about right for this recipe.

7. You can use the gypsum we made earlier in the chapter.

8. Mix everything together until it's evenly combined.

3. Apply a hard squeeze; a small trickle should pour out and stop after a few seconds.

To reach field capacity, add liquid slowly and stir well to ensure an even distribution. Test frequently as you work until you find the right moisture content. If you do accidentally add a bit too much water, this can be remedied with a bit of extra manure or a sprinkle of vermiculite and / or gypsum.

The manure recipe we use is thus:

- 12 parts dry manure
- 6 parts vermiculite
- 1 part gypsum

189

Monotubs allow for much larger mushroom growth.

If you're looking for higher yields, you need a monotub.

Monotubs

A monotub is a dual-purpose incubation and fruiting chamber for your bulk substrate. It's a much simpler construction than your terrarium, as the substrate is so different and doesn't require the same conditions. All you really need from your monotub is enough room to grow a fairly huge amount of mushrooms, a lid that fits and a couple of filtered ventilation holes to allow for adequate air exchange. You'll drill four holes at the casing / substrate level and this will suffice.

Over the years we've modified our monotub design to be more of a mini monotub, or a modified double tub; a real monotub should have sufficient space for the mushrooms to grow without removing the lid. This is easily achieved by buying a tub that's twice as tall as the one we've used. However, we've found that the method we'll describe here has always worked out perfectly with the species that we prefer, *P. cubensis*; the mushrooms seem to grow tall but not excessively so, meaning that you can put the lid on this tub and leave it and all will be well. This is essentially a high-yielding compact grow, giving a very dense, low crop. You do not need a lot of space at all to pull off this type of grow, and it's one of the least effort-in-

This is the fourth flush from this mini monotub!

Once mold appears in your monotub, it needs to be emptied and sterilized.

tensive methods in the whole book. We've prepped and left this many times, and each time it's been a great success. In fact, we've plumb forgotten about it before and discovered it weeks later only to be treated to a fourth or fifth flush of 400 (wet) grams!

We don't case our mini monotub, as casing is a bit of a controversial topic. Many say it can introduce contaminants and trap them onto the substrate, and we feel this isn't a risk we need to take; as you'll see, we've experienced no ill effects from leaving out the casing step. We also advise against casing as you can soak and reuse the substrate a number of times after the first harvest, and this is infinitely more difficult when there's a casing layer that must be removed and reapplied after every soaking. Why make life more difficult?

This method is most definitely not a one-harvest deal. All you need to do after the first flush is harvest the shrooms and soak the substrate in water, then return to the tub. You'll not just get one more flush, nor two—in fact, we've had numerous flushes from every mini monotub, resulting in an average of a kilo and a half of wet shrooms by the time we decide to retire it. A kilo and a half for next to no effort; can you see why we love this method?

Prepping Your Mini Monotub

Your monotub should be plastic and see-through, with a similar lid, and the necessary size will vary according to how much substrate you want to put inside. We used a 5.5 x 10.6 x 5.9 inches size tub (14 x 27 x 15 cm); you can buy these easily and for not a lot of money. As you'll be using this tub a fair amount (grow after grow), it's a good idea to mark two lines all the way around the outside of your tub. These are for marking bulk substrate depth and casing depth (if used). Casing depth should be 25% of your bulk substrate depth; for instance, if your substrate depth is 3 inches, your casing should be three-quarters of an inch deep.

Could this be more beautiful? This is a huge yield.

Some of these shrooms aren't quite as mature as their tub mates.

The perfect mushroom. Not that we have favorites.

Once your monotub is ready and your substrate is pasteurized (which will be explained in the following pages), you will inoculate it using the colonized grain from your grain jars. You can vary the amount used; if you are growing at the start of the season and don't mind waiting for full colonization of the substrate, you can use only a small amount of the colonized grain (around 10% of total volume), saving some for another use. If you are growing at the end of the season and want to colonize the substrate quickly, you can use a larger amount of this colonized grain. Both ways will eventually lead to fully colonized manure and then on to high yields, but it's up to you how quickly you make it happen.

The advantage that a monotub has over a terrarium is that it barely needs any looking after. Once your manure mixture is inoculated, you simply seal the tub and leave it—right until harvest. You should avoid opening up the tub, as this can allow contaminants to infect the grow, meaning that you can literally just leave it alone from inoculation day to harvest day. In addition to this, once the tub is sealed, it should be free from contaminants and should grow without issue. This also means that the mushrooms should be vigorous and well grown, making them good to use for cloning, spore prints and the like. If you've had to use a tub that's not quite big enough to last the whole fruiting period, you can remove the lid and place the whole tub into a fruiting chamber (like the one in Chapter 4) when the mushrooms are reaching the lid.

Making a Mini Monotub

1. Spray the inside of your tub with isopropyl alcohol.

2. Ensure you get the whole inside of the tub and all the corners.

3. Don't forget the outside and lid of the tub.

4. You'll need some heavy-duty garbage bags to line the inside.

5. Cut the bag roughly to size, leaving a little more than you think you'll need.

6. You want a little excess garbage bag but not too much.

7. Push it down into the corners and ensure that it fills the whole tub.

8. Put the lid on the tub and trim the bag flush with the edges of the tub.

9. Tape the bag to the inside walls of the tub.

10. Voila! This is ready to be filled and used.

Double Tubs

The principle of these is much the same as a monotub, except you're using two tubs; one inverted on top of the other to create the same growing space. Depending on the tub you use, you can potentially increase your substrate depth, which should increase the size of your mushrooms and generally improve your yields. All things considered, there's no overall advantage of one method over the other—just two different ways of achieving great yields.

Both tubs are prepared in exactly the same way: four holes at an appropriate level to your chosen substrate depth, plus casing if you're using one. With both tubs prepared in the same way, you can use either one for your bulk substrate. Once this is done, prepare your tubs in the exact same way as you did for monotubs, just sealing with the inverted tub instead of a lid.

Pasteurizing

Pasteurizing is a process that's similar to sterilization, and it works in the same way; using high temperatures to kill off unwanted bacteria. However, pasteurization occurs at a lower temperature than sterilization, and it doesn't

Even if your substrate breaks, mushrooms will continue to grow.

kill off all the bacteria, instead leaving the good stuff behind. This is what happens to milk before it's allowed to be sold to you, and though some would argue that too much good stuff is killed off in the pasteurization process, none can argue that it stops you from getting sick from drinking the white stuff. Sterilization also happens more quickly, by keeping the organic material at 250°F (121°C) for 20 minutes, whereas pasteurization occurs over an hour and requires temperatures of around 175°F (79.4°C).

We use a water-bath sterilization method, as this is the best and most efficient method for small amounts of substrate, and it can also be achieved in your kitchen with equipment that you'll most likely already have or can source without much financial outlay.

We use an old pillowcase to hold the manure in this method, and we've found that this is near perfect as a container for the poo.

It's also worth buying yourself a decent candy thermometer, as this is another thing that will come in handy again and again and will more than prove its worth to you over time.

Once you've pasteurized the manure substrate, leave it to drain overnight, preferably in a clean bathtub or somewhere easy to clean afterwards. Leaving the pillowcase hanging in a clean bath or shower overnight has the added benefit of allowing the manure to drain to the perfect field capacity you're trying to achieve.

Inoculating Your Bulk Substrate with Grain

This is an incredibly simple step in the bulk substrate process. Essentially you (or more accurately, your mycelium) have already done all the hard work; your grain jars should be completely colonized with healthy rhizomorphic growth and they should be practically begging to be used to inoculate something else. All that's required for inoculation of your bulk substrate is to introduce the colonized grain to it and ensure that it's evenly spread; the mycelium will grow towards the new material and will feed off the nutrients in the manure to grow rapidly and vigorously. The speed of the colonization will be dictated by how much colonized grain you add in, as previously mentioned. We generally use a minimum of 10% grain to spawn, but 25% is optimal and should colonize in about a week. Any higher will colonize more quickly, so keep this in mind if you want to speed up your process.

Pasteurizing Your Manure Substrate

1. Put your manure mix into a cotton pillowcase. An old one.

2. Get a big pot that fits the pillowcase and more.

3. If your pot doesn't have a trivet, you can make one using a colander or cake tin.

4. Drop this upside down onto the bottom of the pot.

5. The trivet will stop the pillowcase from burning to the bottom of the pot.

6. Make sure the pillowcase fits in the pot with room to spare.

7. Fill the pot with water. Normal tap water is fine for this.

8. Ensure that the water level just covers the pillowcase.

9. Weigh the pillowcase down so its below the water level.

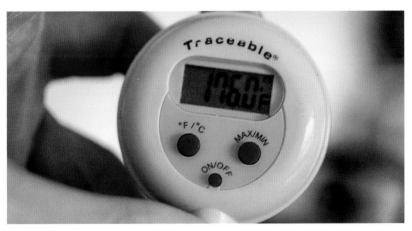

10. Heat the water at 176 degrees Fahrenheit for one hour. Allow to cool completely.

Inoculating Manure from Grain Bags

1. Ensure that your grain bag is fully inoculated, then gently break up the grain.

2. In a still air room, cut open the grain bag. Work as quickly as you can.

3. Put a layer of colonized grain on the bottom of the mini monotub.

4. Grab your sack of shit. It should be well drained.

5. Don't forget to use gloves for this. No one likes poopy hands.

6. Create a layer of your manure substrate on top of the grain layer.

7. Add another layer of inoculated grain. It should just about cover the manure layer.

8. You can spread the grain out evenly to break up clumps.

9. Then add another layer of manure. Pat it down gently if you want to fit more in.

10. You guessed it; it's another layer of inoculated grain!

11. And another manure layer. This layering helps foster even colonization.

12. As you work, make sure there are no clumps. Break them up if there are.

13. Pat the next layer of grain down into the manure. *Continues →*

201

14. Keep going until all your manure is used up.

15. Then add the final layer of inoculated grain.

16. Feel free to mix this up if you really want to. Up to you!

17. Pat everything down to create an even substrate depth.

18. Tape the edges of the garbage bag below the air holes.

19. The air holes should be unobstructed as good airflow is essential.

20. We've marked substrate depth and casing depth on our tub. This is helpful.

21. Tape the whole tub closed to hold the lid in place.

22. We're not sealing out air, but ensuring that the substrate is protected from contaminants.

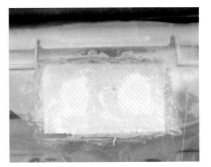

23. Tape another garbage bag around the tub but leave the air holes free.

24. Air holes are easy to make with a large-diameter drill bit, some Tyvek and some glue.

25. Place the tub in a place with good incubation conditions, like an airing cupboard.

Casing

Casing in an optional step in any mushroom bulk technique. The term simply refers to the introduction of a nonnutritious "casing" layer on top of the substrate; we did this in the basic PF Tek when we created a layer of vermiculite on top of the brown rice substrate.

The debate about casing is an ongoing one. Those who swear by casing bulk substrates claim that it brings a number of benefits. First, it helps the substrate to more efficiently hold moisture, meaning that it won't dry out as quickly as it would if there was no casing layer. It's important to keep your substrate from drying out, as mushrooms need water to grow—after all, they're mostly water! Second, the casing layer helps to provide humidity within the substrate, enabling the primordia (those first little runty mushrooms) to form and poke their tiny heads out into the real world. Third, the casing layer provides another line of defense against contaminants that might work their way into your tub, allowing the substrate to stay relatively sterile. Finally, it's argued that casing layers often result in larger flushes of mushrooms, thanks to the ability of the substrate to maintain higher moisture and humidity levels. This wetter condition helps to create the perfect environment in which mushrooms flourish, and the extra bit of effort required to create a casing layer will most definitely pay off in a higher yield; or at least, that's the theory. It's certainly true for other species of non-psychedelic mushrooms, but for *P. cubensis*, the jury is still out.

However, those who argue against the need for casing bulk substrates claim that it is an unnecessary step; a waste of time, money and effort that has the potential to actually damage your grow. The theory goes that the casing layer can trap contaminants and allow them to flourish; you're more likely to get a contaminated bulk substrate with a casing layer than without. The argument about increased yields can be and has been, in our experience, proven wrong by comparing the yields from cased and uncased bulk crops, and indeed if you're going to soak and reuse your substrate, a casing layer can make the whole thing a lot more difficult. We stopped casing our bulk substrate grows a long time ago and they've never been better.

However, like anything in growing, it's really up to you. You might simply prefer it; you might be convinced that it helps your grow. Fair enough; who are we to argue? We don't recommend using a casing layer, but if you choose to, the recipe below is a good one. Casing may be beneficial when

Shrooms will grow up the sides of your tub, even if there's little space.

These shrooms have bent and turned to fit into the corners.

They're not pretty, but they're still potent!

you're unsure about your grow chamber's relative humidity, as it protects your substrate from drying out. If your grow chamber is well humidified however, you may not see much of a difference in yield.

Casing recipes, like everything else in mushroom growing, vary considerably. A common one proposed by Stamets is (by volume):

- 10 parts peat moss
- 1 part gypsum
- 1 part calcium carbonate

Another one is the 50/50+ recipe:

- 31 parts vermiculite
- 31 parts peat moss
- 9 parts crushed oyster shell
- 1 part hydrated lime

We get great growth without casing, so we don't use it.

You will notice that peat moss features predominantly in both these recipes. We don't like using too much peat moss due to some controversy surrounding its conservation status and sustainability. It's argued that the harvesting of peat moss entails a level of habitat destruction that is undesirable, and that peatlands that have been harvested do not naturally return to their former functionality. Peatland restoration requires a number of processes, and even when such areas have been returned to a level close to their former functionality (if they ever are), the photosynthetic rate of the region does not outpace the respiratory rate for a number of years, meaning that the area contributes to the production of greenhouse gases and to climate change overall. Although we can't confirm this, and the debate rages on with passionate arguments from both sides, we err on the side of caution just in case those who argue the above are correct.

Even though this shroom is small, the veil shows that he's ready for picking.

However, peat moss is an undeniably fantastic additive, which is why so many people use it. To avoid using too much of it, we substitute coir for peat moss where possible. Instead of the recipe aforementioned, we use a recipe that relies on Miracle-Gro Moisture Control, which only has a peat moss content of around 50%, and is further diluted with vermiculite to a final concentration of 25% peat moss:

- 19 parts Miracle-Gro Moisture Control
- 19 parts vermiculite
- 2 parts gypsum

This isn't an optimum recipe, as it's slightly nutritious, but we've had decent yields with it. Alternatively, you could forgo casing all together and fruit your bulk substrate directly, as we do.

Like bulk substrates, all casings require pasteurizing. This can be done in jars or in spawn bags, as your volume of casing is only a quarter of your bulk. Fill up your container; if using jars leave the lid off and cover in foil, and if using spawn bags seal with tape.

Making a Casing Layer

1. For this we used 50/50 Miracle-Gro Moisture Control and vermiculite.

2. Add the Miracle-Gro to a large container.

3. Break up any chunks or any debris.

4. Add in the vermiculite, ensuring that it's dry.

5. Mix it gently, making sure that it's evenly combined.

6. Voila. Looks pretty right?

7. Add in water to field capacity. Go slow and add a little at a time.

8. Mix with your hands to ensure it's evenly hydrated.

9. Hold a handful of the mixture lightly. No drips should emerge.

10. Squeeze the mixture hard and a few drips or a trickle should escape.

Continues →

11. If this is the case, your mixture is at field capacity.

12. Load the mixture into a grain bag for pasteurization.

13. Fold the bag to get rid of any excess space.

14. Seal with tape to prevent the bag from springing open.

15. We used autoclave tape to create this neat little package.

16. Stick your candy thermometer right into the middle, then pasteurize.

This is the beginning of a second flush. These will grow much bigger.

Harvest

In monotubs, your bulk substrate will be left alone until harvest time. When will you know it's time to harvest? Well, aren't you glad you bought that see-through tub? As with PF Tek, your perfect harvest time is right as the veil breaks, before the spores start dropping. The difference this time will be that your mushrooms will be considerably larger—stems the length of your forearm and caps the size of saucers are not that uncommon.

Sometimes it can be difficult to remove a mushroom (or, more likely, a cluster of mushrooms) without pulling out a chunk of the substrate, which is not ideal, as you may want to get more flushes out of your substrate. It is possible to cut the mushroom close to the base, leaving the base intact. However, this isn't ideal as the fruit will rot. Even smaller "aborts" will rot

This substrate broke in half, but it has not stopped the mushrooms!

and should be removed from the tub. If you do have to cut your mushroom, be sure to remove the rest of the stump as quickly as possible. When harvesting, if you grab the mushroom at its base and twist as you pull, you should be able to get the whole thing out without causing too much damage to the substrate.

We usually get between 600 and 700 wet grams from the first flush of our mini monotub.

Subsequent Flushes

However, this isn't the end from your monotub. As mentioned above, your monotub will yield several flushes. You can, if you really want to, simply leave it and see what happens; most likely you'll find some shrooms growing but not all that many, and they'll be oddly shaped and strange looking. However, a soak will allow you to get a full-sized second flush from the tub. After you've removed all the mushrooms, gently lift the substrate block out of the tub and place it into water for 12 hours, or overnight. After this time, shake off any excess water and place the substrate back into the tub, then close it up again.

Mushrooms will start to appear fairly quickly, and your resultant yield

Resoaking your manure substrate allows you to get a number of flushes.

can be just as high as your first flush. As the water pools in the bottom of the substrate, you might find that greater clusters grow at the bottom and sides; this is fine. Continue on as normal until the mushrooms are ready to be harvested again. After that, you can soak again; we've had six or more flushes from one single monotub. Over the course of each subsequent flush, the yield may dwindle to half its original size, but as this can total over a kilo and a half of wet shrooms over four or five flushes, this isn't bad at all. If you're still getting over 300 grams from your fourth flush, as we do, you're doing okay.

We re-soaked our substrate just twice and yet still got six or seven flushes off it, despite leaving it in the spare room and only remembering it often enough to harvest each flush. From this semi-abandoned mini monotub, we got an incredible 3 kilos of wet shrooms (300 grams dried).

You'll know when to retire your substrate block; your mushrooms won't be growing properly and it'll be time for a refresh. As the grow continues, the chance of contamination obviously increases. However if you do want to squeeze every drop out of your monotub, feel free to see how far it will go. When it starts to mold or is simply spent, it's time to start all over again!

Agar

If you've become confident enough with the methods already discussed in this book and are looking to take a step forward in purifying your cultures, maintaining your culture line and engaging in methods that feel and look a lot more professional, you'll want to get into agar.

Agar is a gelatinous, nonnutritious substance that's used extensively in labs for a variety of cell culture and microbiology techniques. It's obtained from algae and is sold as a powder, but it can be mixed with hot water and left to set, wherein it forms a fantastic solid medium for mushroom cultures and other things like bacteria. However, agar itself doesn't contain the nutritional material that mycelium need to grow, so it must be combined with another substance that can provide this nutritional content. We've used potato dextrose agar (PDA) in this chapter, which is made from agar mixed with a potato infusion with added dextrose (sugar), though you can also grow fungi on Sabouraud agar, which contains peptones, and malt extract agar, which is particularly good for growing fungi and mold. We use PDA as it's easy to use and widely available; you can buy PDA powder on all the usual online retail vendors for not too much money.

For the home mushroom-grower, agar offers a whole array of benefits. In

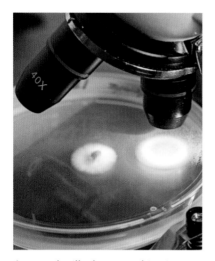

Agar work will take your cultivation skills up a notch. It's also super fun.

labs, agar plates provide a medium on which microorganisms can be grown for observation under a microscope; as agar is indigestible for many microorganisms, the medium stays solid and unchanged while the colony grows over it. While this is also a benefit that home growers enjoy (especially if you have a wicked microscope as we do), you'll mainly use your agar for isolating spores in order to purify cultures, and also in order to clone. Purifying your cultures allows you to rescue healthy growth from contaminated material, and strain isolation uses the same technique in order to isolate the strongest mycelial growth and so optimize your cultures. In both methods, you cut away the desired portion of mycelial growth and transfer it to new, sterile agar plates, where they will flourish.

Agar can also be used to store cultures for later use. Plates can be stored in the fridge, wrapped in Parafilm, for a good few weeks without drying out. However, for long-term storage, agar slants are the top choice. We will discuss this in more detail at the end of this chapter.

This sneaky little guy has managed to grow on a colonized agar plate. Good for him.

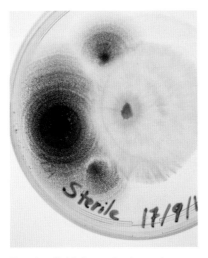

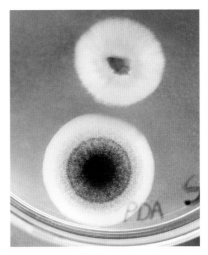

Despite all this bacteria, that culture can still be saved!

Here a contaminant is outgrowing the mushroom tissue!

Pouring Agar Plates

To use agar, you'll need to source some petri dishes with lids. Plastic petri dishes (or "plates") come in lots of different sizes, with features such as extra deep bases or sectioning into halves or thirds. The plates we use are the standard 3.5 inch diameter (90 mm), 0.63 inch (16 mm) depth, and can be easily bought online. Ours come in pre-sterilized "sleeves" of 25 petri dishes in a sealed plastic bag, which is the most common way to buy them. If you buy from a "go-between" vendor who sends your plates loose in an unsealed bag, send them back and buy elsewhere as these will be guaranteed unsterile.

You might also want to consider glass petri dishes, which are more expensive but can be used over and over again, whereas plastic plates are single use only. The glass used to make petri dishes is incredibly heat resistant, meaning that you can sterilize them over and over again with no ill effect. Glass petri dishes will need to be steam sterilized before each use, but they can be filled with the required volume of agar before sterilizing to save time and contamination risk during pouring.

The Prof loves agar work, as it allows for observation of mycelium under a microscope.

Glass petri dishes can be sterilized and reused. However, they can also break.

We use plastic petri dishes for agar work. They're cheap and readily available.

Throughout this book and through our growing careers, we've primarily used plastic petri dishes, and we've found that they suit our purposes perfectly.

As plastic petri dishes can't stand up to the high temperatures needed for proper sterilization, it's easiest to make your PDA in a glass Mason jar, sterilize it in there and then pour your agar plates in a glove box. You can sterilize this jar in your pressure cooker as normal. PDA powder can be bought online and it's incredibly easy to mix into useable agar. Don't be put off by price; a little goes a very long way.

Agar sets at 90–104°F (32°C–40°C), but melts at 185°F (85°C). It's worth keeping these temperatures in mind. If you let your agar cool a bit, it becomes more viscous and easy to pour, but let it cool too much and it will set. To fix this you will have to raise the temperature up to 185°F (85°C) by placing the jar in a pan of hot water and keeping it there for a few hours. You can do this much quicker in a microwave but we do not recommend this. The rapid but uneven heating of a microwave can cause your agar to superheat—this is where it reaches temperatures above 212°F (100°C) without boiling. Superheated agar is very dangerous as releasing the pressure when opening the jar can cause the whole mixture to suddenly boil, running the risk of very severe scalding. If you insist on doing this, keep a constant eye on the microwave and stop every five to ten seconds to swirl the mixture until it's dissolved. However we say again: we do not recommend this! Take your time and use a hot-water bath.

Making Agar

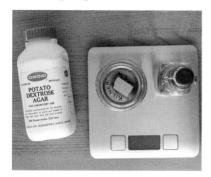

1. You can use any agar mix containing nutritious material. We've used PDA.

2. Weigh out 12 grams of PDA powder into a Mason jar.

3. Add 200 ml of water. This can make up to 30 agar plates (poured thinly).

4. Place the lid tightly on the jar and swirl to mix the powder and water.

5. Your agar is now ready to be sterilized in a pressure cooker.

219

As plastic petri dishes come in a pre-sterilized sleeve, this makes them incredibly easy for home growers to utilize. To use these, tear the end off the bag that corresponds to the base of each plate. Then, holding all the plates together through the bag, place the open end down on your work surface. Gather the top of the bag to release as many plates as you need, using your free hand to guide them out in a stack. Finally, gather the open end and work the unused plates back into the bag, rolling up the opening to keep the plates tightly sealed. This may seem awkward at first, but doing this will help keep your sleeve sterile. Avoid putting your hand into the bag and pulling out plates; you're just loading the bag with contaminants that will later grow when you add agar.

When your agar has cooled enough to be handled, it will be a caramel color and look like runny honey. It's now time to pour your plates. We've performed this with gloves on in an open environment so that you can see how the process is meant to go, but you should perform this in a glove box (or, better, a laminar flow hood if you have access to one). Even in a

Sterilized agar is honey colored and viscous, like this.

Unbagging Plastic Petri Dishes

1. Open the sterile sleeve at the bottom and hold the stack of dishes with one hand.

2. Use your other hand to guide the dishes you need out.

3. Work the unused plates back into the bag and roll up and seal the opening.

glove box you should expect some possibility of contamination, which is why the plates are left for a few days before they're inoculated; by this time, any contaminants will have shown themselves on the medium and you can deal with any affected plates.

When pouring the agar, work as quickly as you can to reduce the chance of contamination. You should pour just enough to cover the bottom of each petri dish; remember that your cultures will grow across the top of the agar, not down into it, so there's no need to have a layer of agar that's more than two-tenths of an inch thick. The less time that the plates spend

Pouring Agar Plates

1. Ensure that you've got enough space to work quickly and smoothly.

2. Loosen the lid of the agar Mason jar and put it in your dominant hand.

3. Remove the Mason jar lid only when you're ready to star pouring.

4. Quickly lift all dishes but the bottom one, along with the lid of the bottom dish.

5. Pour a thick layer of agar two-tenths of an inch thick. It should cover the whole dish.

6. Put the rest of the stack and the lid down to close the bottom dish.

7. Lift up all dishes but the next one, including the lid to open it. Pour again.

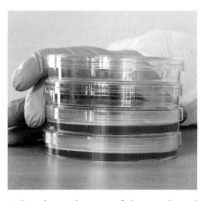

8. Put down the rest of the stack and the lid to close the second dish.

9. Repeat this process, working as quickly as possible each time.

10. Don't make the agar layer thicker than two-tenths of an inch. It's just a waste of agar.

11. Keep going until all the plates are poured, then secure the lid on the agar jar.

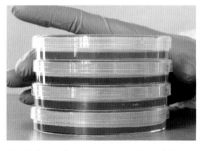

12. Refrain from opening the plates until you're ready to use them.

open, the better. When you've poured plates a few times you'll get into the habit of working upwards from the bottom of a stack, as we've illustrated in these photos. To pour your first plate, take all dishes except the bottom one in your non-dominant hand. Make sure that you've grabbed the lid of the bottom plate, too. When you lift the stack (and the lid), pour enough agar into the plate, then quickly put the rest of the stack (and the lid) down to close the bottom jar. Repeat this process, pouring the next plate up every time until all plates are poured. We are aware that this sounds complicated, and we will concede it's far easier to show than explain. There's a whole section of YouTube that has lots of great videos on how to do basic laboratory techniques like this; if our instructions are confusing, have a search and see what you can find.

Although you want to pour your plates relatively thinly (a few tenths of a fluid ounce is fine), there are some times when you might want to pour in extra. Deeper agar means slower drying times, which is useful if you're making plates to be used a few weeks later or to store a strain for a similar amount of time.

We used 12 grams of PDA powder in 200 ml (around three-quarters of a cup) of water, which can make up to 30 plates if you pour thinly enough. If you're unsure, follow the instructions provided by your agar supplier; however, if you use slightly more agar than suggested on the packaging, it makes it slightly more viscous and easier to work with.

Your plates should set in five to 10 minutes, at which point you will need to seal them with Parafilm. This is a type of breathable but waterproof lab film made from paraffin plastic that is ductile, translucent and able to withstand the high temperatures needed for sterilization. For these reasons, it's used to seal agar plates against contamination and to slow the drying process. Parafilm isn't too expensive and is widely available from online retailers. If you're doing agar work, it's an absolute godsend. After you've sealed your plates, leave them in a room of a similar temperature as your grow for a few days to check for contamination. This prevents you from wasting time inoculating contaminated plates and is the reason you should always make a few more plates than you think you'll need. Working in a glove box is bound to introduce some contaminants, and after a few plate-pouring sessions many growers can come up with a fairly stable loss-adjustment system to help them decide how many extra plates they should pour.

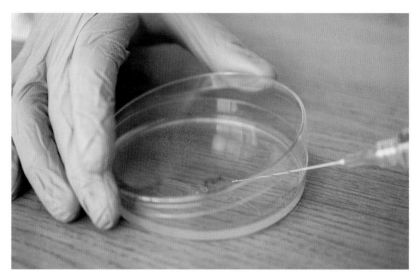

To inoculate agar, simply lift the lid and squirt a little spore solution / liquid culture inside.

Inoculating Your Agar Plates

You can introduce living material to an agar petri dish in a number of ways. The first is with spores; if you're working with a spore syringe, you simply lift the petri dish lid (inside a glove box, of course), squirt some of the spore suspension in an "S" shape on top of the agar and close the lid again, sealing with Parafilm before you bring the dishes out of the glove box. One or two drops of this liquid is more than enough, and using the needle to gently spread an "S" shape allows for lots of different germination points. The second is with liquid culture, which is achieved in much the same way. The third is to transfer already living material onto the agar; that is, through cloning. This involves taking a piece of that material, whether it's an already-colonized piece of agar, a kernel of grain or a tissue sample from a freshly picked mushroom from your previous grow and dropping it onto the agar plate, preferably in the middle. The mycelium will grow outwards towards the edge of the dish until the plate is fully colonized.

Cloning from Mushroom Tissue

If you are partway through a grow and are starting to consider where your next mushrooms are going to come from, you might want to consider cloning on agar. This is an incredibly simple but highly reliable and effective way to maintain a culture and use your living material to inoculate new substrates, rather than going back to spores or liquid culture. Cloning involves taking a piece of pure material from the mushroom and depositing it on the agar medium, where it can feed off the nutrients in the PDA solution and grow.

It's actually slightly better to choose young mushrooms as your donors, as mushrooms in the early stages of life are in a state of vigorous cell division and can recover quickly and easily from the shock of transfer; that is, from having been cut away from their growing medium and placed on a new medium. However, there's absolutely nothing wrong with using a mature mushroom, and the differences between their rate of growth post cloning probably won't be an issue for you. Older mushrooms are also said to be more prone to contamination, but if you follow good practice and sterile technique you should minimize this possibility.

When choosing a mushroom for cloning, pick one that looks healthy and strong; remember that you'll be cloning this tissue, so you want to choose a donor that has the traits you want to recreate. It's imperative to use freshly picked mushrooms for this process; while you can store your mushrooms for three to four days and then clone from them, it's much more difficult to find viable tissue and the success rate will be low. Clone immediately after you've picked the mushroom and your success rate will be high. You'll tear your chosen mushroom in half (cutting with a scalpel can drag surface contaminants across your otherwise axenic cloning site) and then cut from one of two locations: the area directly below the cap or the fat base of the stem. These areas give the most successful clones. As ever, you should use a flame-sterilized scalpel for this technique, and you should perform this method inside a glove box (or laminar flow hood if you have access to one).

On agar, mycelium will grow outwards, towards the edge of the petri dish.

How to Clone From a Mushroom

1. Pick a strong, healthy-looking mushroom and clean it with Tyvek or a clean cloth.

2. Wipe both the stalk and caps gently but thoroughly.

3. Starting at the bottom of the stalk, tear it apart like so.

4. Slowly keep going until the whole mushroom is split in two.

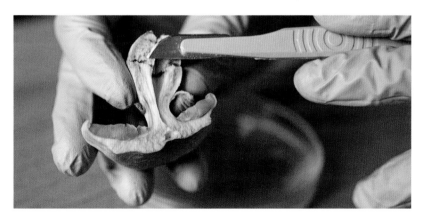

5. You can choose to cut a clone from either the fat base of the stem …

Continues →

6. ... or directly below the cap. These sites give successful clones.

7. Using a sterile scalpel, gently cut away a small piece of the mushroom.

8. It doesn't need to be any bigger than this. One mushroom can give many clones.

9. Grab your sterile agar plate and gently lift the lid.

10. Quickly place the mushroom piece into the very center of the agar plate.

11. Pull away the scalpel and close the lid as quickly as possible.

12. Cut a piece of Parafilm to size and tear away the backing paper.

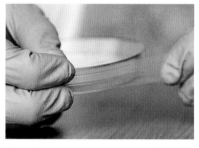

13. Hold one edge of the Parafilm over the petri dish seam with one hand.

14. Stretch the Parafilm outwards and around the edge of the petri dish.

15. Stick the Parafilm to itself to properly seal the dish. Done!

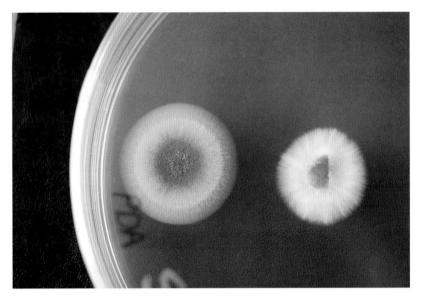

Agar work allows you to isolate contaminants and therefore purify cultures.

Of course, one mushroom can give a number of clones. Paul Stamets recommends a minimum of 10 repetitions when cloning, but you can do as many as you see fit for your needs. In a few days, you'll start to see new mycelial growth pushing outwards from the clone. You'll also start to see evidence of contamination if there is any.

If you do find contaminated clones, do not throw them away in despair just yet! Through a rapid series of agar transfers, you can effectively outrun your contamination problem in the same manner as you do when purifying cultures (see section on Purifying Cultures later in this chapter). However, this only works for instances of small contamination; if your contamination is extensive it might be best to simply start again rather than potentially release contaminants into your glove box and general growing area.

Cloning does, however, have some downsides. If you clone from a mushroom, grow out that strain, clone from the resulting mushrooms, then repeat this cycle, you will be moving further and further away from your original source material. No new genetic material will be introduced; you will simply be working with the same strain. Over time, this will result in issues like slowed growth, low yields, anemic-looking mushrooms and a general lack of vigor in your cultivation. This is called senescence, or

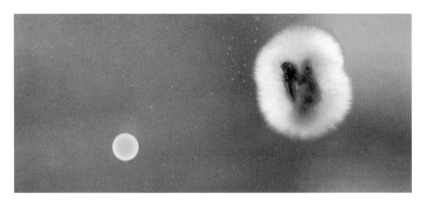

Here you can see a small bacteria spot on the agar plate.

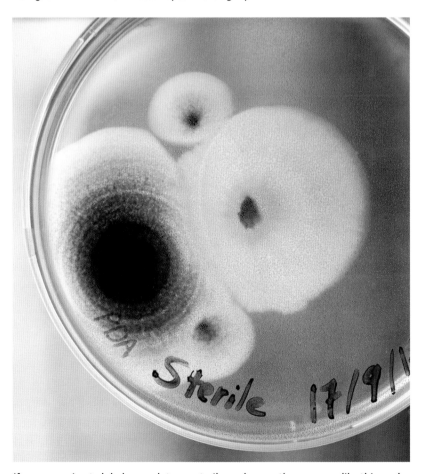

If you are going to label your plates as sterile, make sure they are—unlike this one!

Mother Nature's handiwork on display.

biological aging. As humans we also experience senescence; it's why your skin has less elasticity as you grow older, or why your bones become more brittle, or why your hair just gets thinner and thinner until it starts to fall out entirely. As the wonderful grower and online mushroom educator Roger Rabbit analogized, you can feed an old man highly nutritious food but it won't reverse the aging process. If you have cloned from the same line over and over, it will get old. For this reason, it's a good idea to rely on a mixture of cloning, liquid culture and growing from your own spore prints. Switch between the three of these and you'll soon be a self-sufficient little mushroom farmer with a vigorous and reliable grow.

Purifying Cultures

Whether you're working with cultures that have originated from spores or from living tissue, they can pick up contaminants on the way to your grow. You might, for instance, have sourced a questionable spore syringe from a friend, and you may be unsure as to whether it is still viable. Working with agar allows you to clean up or purify these cultures so you can continue working with them; it's a great screening technique for bad cultures or contaminated spores.

Agar corers make it easy to transplant pieces of colonized agar.

Contaminants will show themselves within a few days of inoculation of your agar plates. As mycelial growth is quite uniform and linear (at least from *P. cubensis*), it can be easy to spot any growth that is suspiciously different from that exhibited by your culture. Dark spots, slimy areas or anything that's not white can be considered a sign of contamination. When the contaminant grows, it will battle the mycelium for dominance of the plate, which can result in some fascinating little agar wars, though it's not good news for your mycelium. However, you can easily transfer the healthy, uncontaminated mycelium into a new plate and therefore save it.

Before you begin the transfer, choose which portion of the agar you're going to cut and move to a new petri dish. It's a good idea to transfer from the leading edge of the colony, where cell division is occurring rapidly. This allows the transferred piece to retain its vigor and quickly grow on the next plate. If there have been any bacteria on your plate, choose a healthy, strong-looking piece of growth on a leading edge that's far away from the bacteria spot. You only need a small piece of colonized agar, so even if there are several bacteria spots, you can simply work around them.

Mold poses more of an issue than bacteria when purifying your cultures, as mold spores are airborne and therefore can hitch a ride on your transferred material without you knowing. For this reason, you should perform your material transfer in a glove box, flow hood or still air environment. However, if transfer of mold spores does occur, you can simply continue transferring the mycelium to new agar plates until sterility is achieved.

A piece of dried shroom on a glass petri dish, ready to go under the microscope.

In your glove box or still air environment, open up the petri dish and quickly but carefully use a flame-sterilized scalpel to cut away a piece of the agar containing only healthy mycelial growth. Quickly and carefully lift this piece of agar out of the contaminated plate, close the plate and place the piece of agar in the middle of a new, sterile plate. That's it. Ensure that the new petri dish is sealed with Parafilm and label it as per

The gills of the mushroom drop spores, ensuring a new generation of shrooms.

your labeling system to ensure that no confusion occurs later on. As with any contaminated material, you should seal the contaminated agar plate and dispose of it properly and safely.

Agar corers, also known as cork borers, are a great way to take quick samples of mycelium to transfer cultures to many new plates. They often come in a set of various sizes and can be bought cheaply online. To use them, simply select an appropriate size, flame until hot, then use to quickly punch a series of circles in the desired area. Once this is done, replace the petri lid and sterilize a scalpel or tweezers. Finally, use your scalpel or tweezers to transfer each disk to a new plate.

We prefer this method to using just a scalpel as it's much quicker and easier. Also you spend less time with your plates open while you try to cut out a section of mycelium, reducing the chance of contamination.

When transferring, always consider making a few extra plates if you can. This helps minimize the chance of contaminants ruining everything. We typically transfer one plate to three to five new agar plates, using different sections of mycelium. If only one survives without contamination you've still succeeded!

Some growers may talk about using antibiotics such as gentamicin to fight off contaminants. Whilst this is an option, we prefer good sterile technique. Antibiotics are expensive and most are rendered useless by autoclaving (gentamicin is one exception, though it requires lower temperatures). Also, most are selective, meaning they only target bacteria or molds. They have some value in purifying wild cultures, which are often loaded with all kinds of microorganisms, but for the home *P. cubensis* grower they're mostly an unnecessary expense.

Strain Isolation

When we talk about strains in mycology, we refer not to different types of mushroom (as cannabis cultivators use the word), but to the strains that result from individual spores mating. These strains will start to show as the mycelial growth reaches an inch or so away from its starting point in the middle of the agar plate. They appear as thicker strands of white growth, and you'll notice that some seem to be growing more quickly than others. Using the same methods as detailed above, the mushroom grower can isolate strains that look particularly strong and vigorous, and transfer

The thread like mycelial growth indicates that this is a good plate to clone from.

This plate has been cloned, as it shows good, strong rhizomorphic growth.

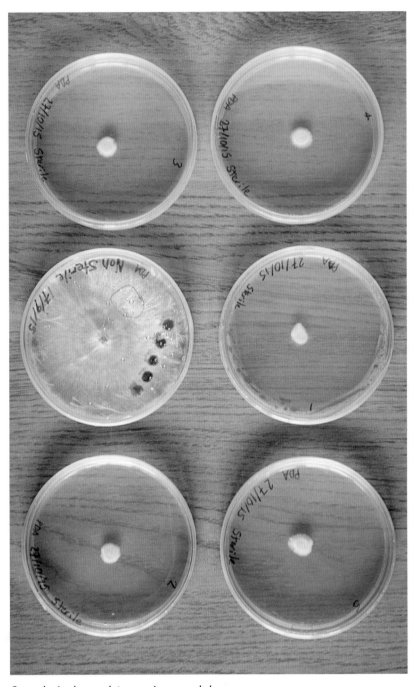

One colonized agar plate can give several clones.

these to new agar plates for further cultivation and use. This is known as strain isolation and can be a great way to optimize your culture (and cut down the amount of time it takes for your mushrooms to grow when they've been transferred to a bulk substrate).

The technique used for strain isolation is much the same as the one previously mentioned. Sterile practice must be maintained, or you risk contaminating a healthy culture. Cut away the section of agar that contains the strongest-looking strain and quickly transfer this out of the agar plate and onto a new sterile one. It's best to cut a transfer from the outer edge of the growing culture; these edges are called the hyphal tips of the mycelium. It's also best to perform transfers before the culture has reached the edge of your petri dish. If you perform a transfer as soon as you can identify the strong strain that you'd like to work with, this minimizes the number of cell divisions that have already occurred. Again, seal the new agar plate with Parafilm and label it properly.

Picking a Good Strain— Rhizomorphic Versus Tomentose

As we discussed in Chapter 1, mycelium show two types of growth; rhizomorphic and tomentose. The former is a stringy-looking, fast-growing form that grows outwards from the inoculation point like a tree, forming individual branches as it goes. The latter is a fluffy, cloud-like type that grows a lot more slowly and can often be confused for contamination. Most types of mushroom will exhibit tomentose mycelial growth before the rhizomorphic growth shows itself, but the rhizomorphic growth is where the mushroom fruits will eventually spring from, and it's for this reason that, as home growers, we want to cultivate as much rhizomorphic growth as we can.

Rhizomorphic growth occurs when strands of mycelium begin growing in parallel, seeking out nutrients that it can transfer to the rest of the colony. The process of separating rhizomorphic growth from tomentose growth is called sectoring, and it allows the home grower to develop a stronger culture that will eventually yield more highly and grow more rapidly. Using the strain isolation technique above, this is a relatively simple procedure. Always choose the thickest, most vigorous-looking rhizomorphic strain and avoid any fluffy or weak-looking growth. It's the tomentose growth that you want to leave behind.

Inoculating Grain Jars with Colonized Agar

1. Grab a prepared grain jar and an agar plate showing vigorous growth.

2. If there's contamination on your plate, mark it so you can avoid it.

3. Heat the scalpel blade over a flame, keeping it red for a few seconds.

4. Lift the lid and touch the blade to the agar to cool it quickly.

5. Quickly but carefully cut from the center of the plate to the edge.

6. Repeat this action a few degrees over, creating a wedge of agar.

7. Place the blade under the wedge and lift it away from the agar plate.

8. Place the lid back on the agar plate as soon as possible.

9. Lift the lid of the grain jar and quickly drop the agar wedge into it.

10. Replace the lid on the grain jar. The wedge will be sitting atop the grain.

11. Secure all parts of the lid and make sure it has ventilation holes.

12. Shake the jar to move the agar wedge further into the grain. And you're done!

Storing Cultures on Agar Slants

1. Pre-poured agar plates are essential for this process. Agar corers are useful but not necessary.

2. Remove the Parafilm from one of your colonized agar plates.

3. Hold the slant in your non-dominant hand and remove the lid with your dominant hand.

4. Cut a piece of agar from the edge of the mycelium with a scalpel or a corer.

5. Keeping hold of the slant and the lid, lift up the piece of agar with your scalpel.

6. Quickly place the agar piece into the agar slant, right onto the agar.

7. Make sure the agar piece is touching the surface of the agar in the tube.

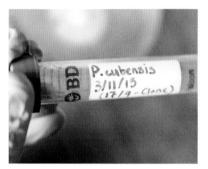

8. Replace the tube's lid quickly and grab a marker to label the slant.

9. Write the species, the date and any other useful information.

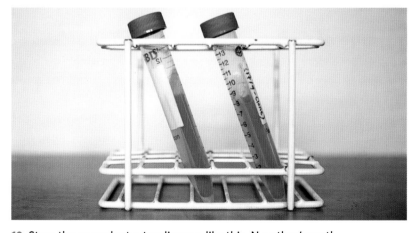

10. Store the agar slants standing up, like this. Now they're set!

Agar Transfers

Once you've grown out a strain on an agar plate and the mycelium have shown fantastic growth, you can start thinking about using that culture. It's incredibly easy to inoculate with agar; you've already got your sterile, uncontaminated material, so all you really need to do is introduce it to a sterile, prepared substrate and wait for it to do its thing.

In order to cut away a piece of colonized agar you'll need a sharp, flame-

sterilized scalpel. Ideally you want a plate that's free from contamination, but this isn't always possible. If there has been any bacteria on your plate, choose a healthy, strong-looking piece of growth that's far away from the bacteria spot. You really only need one small wedge of colonized agar to inoculate an entire grain jar, but the more mycelial material you place into the jar, the more quickly colonization will occur.

Good labeling is absolutely essential for a professional grow op.

If you're looking for speed over thriftiness with your colonized agar, feel free to place two or even three wedges of colonized agar into your sterilized grain jars.

As ever, you should be performing this action in a glove box, but we've done it outside of a glove box to ensure that you can see what's going on.

Storage of Cultures

If you want to store your cultures for later use, agar is a great way to do this. As mentioned earlier, plates can be poured deep and will last a few weeks wrapped in Parafilm.

However, the best way to store cultures is on slants. These are tubes made of glass or heat-resistant plastic that have been partially filled with hot liquid-agar, sterilized and allowed to set at an angle (30–45 degrees). This provides a small surface area that not only prevents the culture from growing too large, but also reduces the evaporative surface and prevents the sample from drying out. Once inoculated, these slants can create a "save point" for your culture that will be good for a year or two. When reanimating

This mushroom has grown on an agar plate! Good work, mushroom.

these cultures, it's always good practice to test their vitality by "plating them out" onto fresh agar plates to look for healthy growth. This prevents you wasting time expecting a grain jar to grow when the culture could have become too old.

When storing your cultures it is best to store them in a fridge. However, it's worth noting that fridge temperatures can swing all over the place, causing condensation to build up, which can pull moisture from your plates and ruin your samples. To avoid this, place your plates / slants in a sealable plastic box before refrigerating. This will stabilize any temperature swings and reduce the chance of condensation.

When picking an area of the fridge, avoid lower shelves and the door. Lower shelves have a higher risk of contaminants falling on them from above, and doors have wider swings in temperature due to their constant opening and closing. Keep your fridge clean, or if you really get into agar work, invest in a small second fridge like we have and use it to keep your mycology materials and nothing else. Truth be told we also keep our bottles of home brew in there too, but we try not to subculture while under the influence.

Troubleshooting and Contaminants

Prevention Is Better than Cure

There's really nothing more annoying than investing a bunch of time and money into a grow and then having to throw the whole thing away because you got a month into it and woke up one day to find the whole shebang was moldier than a college student's laundry basket. It's frustrating as well as a waste of time and money. For this reason, it's worth following basic sterilization methodologies and ensuring that you don't do anything stupid to compromise your grow. Read and reread the best practice methods we outlined in Chapter 3. Also, use your common sense (we know you've got some), and use Google to learn from others' mistakes. You should store grain jars and any other live materials above knee level: two to three feet off the floor or higher. At ground level, it's basically a swamp of contaminants that gets stirred up every time you walk by, and that's a surefire way to get these contaminants into your jars. Keep them at chest height and above and you'll greatly improve your chances.

Types of Mold

Your primary concern when growing mushrooms will always be mold. Sterile substrates are the perfect open environment for mold to grow, if it can

Turn the gloves of the glove box outwards like this when not in use.

When using a glove box, wipe everything with a 10% bleach solution before use.

get in there. Once it's in there, the grow is done. Some people will tell you that you can kill off bits of mold growth with hydrogen peroxide, but as you are going to consume the mushrooms that you grow, we wouldn't recommend trying. Once mold has gotten hold in one of your jars or bags, throw it out. Start again, paying more attention to sterilization methods, environment, inoculation and care after inoculation. Don't fuck around with your health.

Blue-Green Mold: *Penicillium spp.*

This type of mold is particularly fast growing and will present as a quite dense, felt-like covering all over the substrate. It usually presents in various shades of green, though it can also appear white. There are hundreds of different species of *Penicillium*, one of which you'll know as the source of the antibiotic—though this doesn't in any way imply that it's safe to consume. This type of mold is one of the most common in a home mushroom grow, on agar plates and in grain jars and bags specifically, and you should get it out of your grow space immediately once you've identified it.

This one almost made it but got overtaken by blue mold.

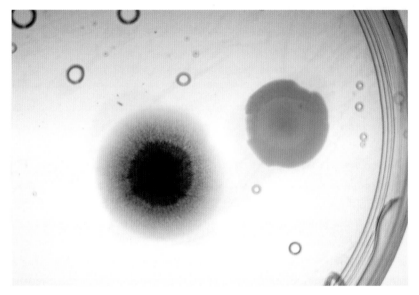

Here we have Trichoderma *(green mold) on the left and bacteria on the right.*

Green Mold: *Trichoderma harzianum*

This type of mold is a particularly nasty little critter, as it is parasitic; that is, it will attack and take nutrition from other types of fungi, including your precious shrooms. It can also be difficult to identify at first, as it begins life as white mycelium much like the ones you're actually trying to grow. However, *Trichoderma* will grow incredibly quickly and grow up onto the mushrooms, causing decay and covering everything in an emerald-green fuzz. Once you've seen it, ditch the affected container. It's most likely to be found on casing layers and in straw.

Cobweb Mold: *Hypomyces spp.*

Another one in the "well that looks annoyingly like mushroom mycelium" genre is cobweb mold, which can remain hidden in plain sight for a good long while before you realize that it's got a solid foothold in your grow. Cobweb mold grows over casing or on cakes and will eventually engulf a mushroom and cause rot. You should look out for mycelium that looks slightly gray compared to mushroom mycelium and strands of growth that seem much more fine than the thick strands of mushroom mycelium. Cobweb mold can take over an entire jar in just a day or so, so be vigilant.

Black Mold: *Aspergillus spp.*

Also shown as both yellow and green in color, black mold is nothing to mess around with. It's easy to confuse this type of mold with *Penicillium*, but black mold is a lot more potentially harmful to you than most others. When the pathogenic *Aspergillus* spores are inhaled, they can cause respiratory problems and pain in the chest, and without treatment can go on to cause even greater problems with kidneys and lungs. Black mold can grow on almost any substrate, though you're most likely to find it on agar plates and in grain cultures. Be incredibly cautious when disposing of black mold-infested materials and use a dust mask to ensure that you don't breathe anything in. And it should go without saying that you would never dispose of such materials in a place where they might pose a risk to others.

Olive-Green Mold: *Chaetomium spp.*

Much as the name suggests, this type of mold will appear as an olive-green fuzz over your substrate, though it's more commonly found on compost and on composted materials. *Chaetomium* spores are heat tolerant and can be a source of dangerous infection in immunocompromised people (kids, the elderly, pregnant women and anyone with an immune disease), so be careful when handling and disposing of it.

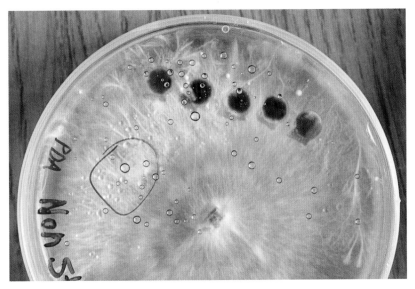

A suspected contamination site has been marked on this agar dish.

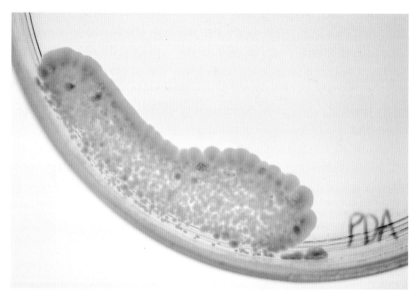

The pink spots here mean this is most likely Geotrichum, *a type of fungi.*

Lipstick Mold: *Geotrichum spp.*

A red or pink growth that will begin life almost white and mature through red to finally become a subdued orange color, this mold is relatively easy to identify and doesn't grow quickly, so it won't take over an entire jar before you've noticed it's there. It will colonize casings but is somewhat uncommon, occurring only when your sterilization procedures are seriously lacking.

How to Properly Dispose of Mold-Infected Materials

Mold is no joke. Some types of mold can be seriously detrimental to your health, and all types can be detrimental to your shrooms. Moreover, if mold spores spread in your home and around your work area, it can totally scupper your next attempts to grow, as the space will already be contaminated and will contaminate your jars or other growing materials. If a jar is heavily contaminated with mold, you should sterilize the jar before you open it; that is, pressure-cook it again. This will kill mold spores. After this, empty the contents outside into a compost pile or flowerbed. If you can't be bothered with that, just dispose of the entire jar and buy a new one. Plastic petri

The pink moisture in the foreground here is most likely Geotrichum.

The overly wet popcorn grain bag is contaminated and needs to be disposed of.

dishes and syringes will melt in the pressure cooker, so put these in a spawn bag and loosely seal before sterilizing. Don't dispose of potentially danger-ous materials anywhere they might pose a danger to others.

Wet Spot: *Bacillus spp.*

No one likes wet spot. It's gross, it stinks and it's disgustingly slimy. You're most likely to find *Bacillus* on grain spawn, where it can sometimes form heat-resistant endospores and therefore survive the sterilization process. You'll notice it first as a grey ooze on uncolonized grain. The medium will appear to be too wet. *Bacillus* can make it through the sterilization process as heat-resistant endospores, which is hardly fair if you ask me. If you're brave enough to take the lid off the affected jars, be ready for an over-whelming smell of rotten fruit or a pile of garbage that's been out in the hot sun too long. Get rid of all affected materials.

Bacterial Blotch: *Pseudomonas spp.*

Once your mushrooms have started to properly form, you might think that you're out of the woods—but no! *Pseudomonas* here likes to occur at a later

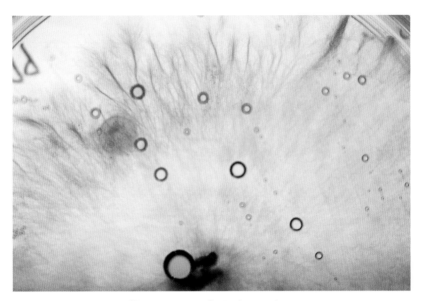

Here you can see a spot of bacteria on a colonized agar plate.

stage, appearing on the caps of the developing mushrooms. Yellow-brown lesions will start to form, typically near the edge of the caps. The affected areas will seem to be slimy in places and will begin to decompose, creating a truly awful smell. Bacterial blotch generally occurs when mushrooms have been wet for too long or when air exchange is not sufficient. This may occur when you are drying your freshly picked shrooms. A humid environment will encourage bacterial blotch, so ensure good air exchange and use a de-humidifier if you experience this problem when drying.

Fungus Gnats

The long-time enemy of cannabis growers, fungus gnats are also partial to feeding on mycelium and will take over mushrooms that are developing and ones that have developed, causing soft rot. They can also carry a number of other diseases that would be catastrophic for your grow. Fungus gnats occur when your growing environment isn't airtight; as a result they are very common in most fruiting chambers. They can also survive outside of your terrarium in the moist soil of houseplants. Good control measures include fly paper and removing houseplants from your grow area—never use insecticide, as these can render you grow toxic and inedible. Another method is to use a biocontrol agent, *Steinernema carpocapsae*; this nematode worm lives inside your substrate and eats the larvae of fungus gnats. However, in reality, fungus gnats are not a problem for the otherwise careful grower and is considered to be a minor annoyance.

Mites

More than being a contaminant themselves, mites and fungus gnats are vectors for contaminants; essentially, they'll bring in foreign materials on their dirty little feet. Mites are most likely to enter your grow on material such as straw and manure, and though they're usually of some assistance to mushrooms when they're growing out in the wild, you don't want them in your house or in your grow. Mites feed on *Penicillium* and *Trichoderma* mold, so they may occur in association with these. A good way to control these is to put your substrates, jars and plates on a sheet of sticky-backed paper. This prevents mites from moving between your cultures, allowing you to isolate and dispose of mite-ridden samples.

Yeast

Yeast is distinct from mold in that it is a single-cell fungus, whereas mold contains multiple identical nuclei. Where mold is fuzzy, yeast appears more

This looks like Geotrichum *is being invaded by* Trichoderma.

threadlike. Whereas mold can present as any of the colors previoulsy described, yeast is usually white, and if you have a yeast contamination in your grow, it will look oval in shape. Yeast can appear after performing grain-to-grain transfers. Look for little white spots all over everything.

The Six Vectors of Contamination

Avoiding contamination necessitates recognition of both the source of contaminants and the vectors (or pathways) through which they travel. As ever, we're grateful to Paul Stamets for his fantastic work on this topic. A huge amount of our understanding on this subject comes from Chapter 10 of his book *Growing Gourmet and Medicinal Mushrooms* and we'd recommend it to any serious mushroom grower.

In order to create a truly sterile environment, it's important to address each one of these vectors.

When psilocybin mushrooms are handled, they bruise blue. This is normal.

These jars have been contaminated by a number of beasties. Throw them out.

1. The Cultivator

That's you, bucko! You're a veritable hotbed of contaminants (sorry not sorry); just think of the many different types of yeast, fungi, bacteria and viruses that love to set themselves up in the warm and comforting inner and outer environments of your body. You might get sick only once or twice a year, but the viruses that cause those illnesses lie dormant in your body for a long while, just waiting until your immune system is compromised and they can take over.

While skin-borne contaminants are the most obvious danger to the sterility of your mushroom set up (and the reason you should wear gloves), you can also spread contaminants through breathing—although we don't recommend that you stop—and through the plethora of different tissue types that you secrete (hair, skin, etc.). There's not much that can be done about this, but you can cut down on the amount of potential contaminants you carry into your work area by changing into clean clothes before working with

Wear gloves to stop you from spreading your filthy germs.

your cultures, tying up your hair, wearing gloves, allowing the air to settle before you begin work and, if it makes you feel better, wearing a surgical mask, though this really just makes you look hilarious.

If you're ill, you're compromising the sterility of whatever you're working on, so give yourself a rest until you're better.

Using the correct type of lid will ensure a successful and uncontaminated grow.

2. The Air

It's everywhere, and it's full of stuff to ruin your mushrooms. Your home is basically a swamp of airborne contaminants. As we've mentioned before, each time you walk around, you stir up the sea of floor-level particles and push them all over the place, which is why you should never keep any materials, jars, agar plates, monotubs or terrariums near the ground. In a lab situation, there are (ideally) at least three doors between the outside and the lab, but this isn't something you can maintain in your home unless you have at least one room solely dedicated to mushroom growing and a, frankly, odd amount of doorways.

The best you can do in your home is turn your bathroom into a still air environment for any processes that you can't do inside a glove box (or flow hood, but we're going to assume that you don't have access to one of those). As we outlined in Chapter 3, this is achieved by using a 10% bleach solution in a spray bottle. First, remove any towels, toilet paper, sponges or shower mats from the bathroom, as well as anything else that's a bit gross. Wipe down any dusty or dirty surfaces and close the toilet lid. Starting at the furthest point from the door, spray a semi-obnoxious amount of this bleach spray high into the air, walking backwards as you do so. When you reach the door, let the mist settle, and as it does so it should, in theory, pin some of the airborne contaminants to the floor. Move gently to your work area (we often use the toilet cistern lid and the toilet lid itself, but make sure they're clean) and work quickly.

3. The Media

Not the newspaper press (although we all know they're dirtier than a Las Vegas strip club floor), but the medium upon which your culture is grown. No matter whether it's grain, manure, agar, brown rice flour or any other substrate, insufficient sterilization or pasteurization will allow contaminants to subsist on your medium and compromise it.

While you might read that sterilization is sufficient at 20 minutes using 15 psi or 250°F (121°C), it can be worth keeping the material at that temperature and pressure for longer (say, 30 to 40 minutes) to ensure that the endospore-forming bacteria present in some additives are rendered benign. However, if you're not adding any additives not mentioned in this book, 20 minutes should be fine. One exception to this advice is when working with liquid media with sugars that may caramelize from prolonged heating, which should always be sterilized for no longer than 20 minutes.

This mold is on a monotub, but it's fairly well contained for now.

Pasteurization, however, takes a little longer, as the temperature is lower. For this, we'd recommend keeping your substrate at 175°F (79.4°C) for an hour, unless you're adding additional nutrients—in which case, increase the time. Be sure to keep the temperature as close to that level as possible; too high and you drift into sterilization temperature, too low and you won't effectively pasteurize—leaving too many contaminants viable.

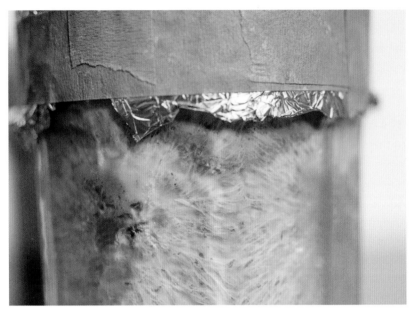

Sometimes mold can hide under the rim of your foil. Keep watch for it!

If you're really looking to dial in your methods, it's a good idea to take a small portion of each sterilized material and leave it uninoculated. This will allow you to see whether it grows mold without the influence of the spores, meaning that you can be sure whether or not the sterilization was successful if you encounter an issue later on. If your inoculated material is contaminated but your uninoculated material isn't, you can be reasonably sure that the issue came from somewhere else, such as your technique or your culture line.

4. The Tools

A bad workman may blame his tools, but sometimes he's right; it is their fault. Almost everything you use in your set up can be a vector for contamination, and because many of your tools will come into direct contact with your culture or its substrate, this can be an issue. We've talked extensively about the need for proper sterilization of work areas and tools, such as wiping down the inside of glove boxes and using fresh syringes. Anything that's made of stainless steel (scalpels, tweezers, agar corers) can be wrapped in foil and pressure-cooked to sterilize. This should be at the forefront of your mind always. Flame sterilization of needles is the method that we use, though you can disinfect them with alcohol. We use alcohol to disinfect throughout the book, too. Although the inside of your pressure cooker may be sterile, it's worth remembering that the outside isn't. You can transfer contaminants from the outside in.

5. The Inoculum

Your inoculum is the culture-containing medium. That can be the spore solution, colonized grain, tissue culture or liquid culture. If your inoculum is contaminated, it will affect whatever you introduce it to. As we've shown with the non-sterile agar plates in Chapter 10, the contaminants introduced can often grow faster and with more vigor than the mycelium, meaning that it can be difficult and time consuming to try to isolate them from your materials. This is possible, though, as we've shown, but it's far better to ensure that your inoculum is properly sterile before you start. If you're using spore syringes bought from an outside source, you're simply going to have to trust their methods, whereas a homemade liquid culture can be sterilized properly and keep you going for a good long while. Relying on your own inoculum rather than ones bought from other sources will always be better.

This non-sterile spore solution on agar shows the contaminants within.

6. Mobile Contamination Units

This is really just a fancy way of describing anything alive that moves of its own volition. This includes mites, houseflies, ants, children, cats and your pet snake. As well as the obvious ethical concerns of placing your children in an environment where currently illegal and always hallucinogenic materials are present, the fact is that both children and pets are petri dishes of disease and incredibly inviting transportation methods for all sorts of contaminants. Worse, though, are the flies and mites that can get into your terrariums or monotubs. They absolutely love warm and humid environments and actively seek out fungi, so if you're having a mushroom party they'll make sure to RSVP.

If you have house pets, it's a good idea to always keep them out of any room that you might use as a workspace—and to avoid touching them or any of their toys before you do anything with your mushrooms.

Of course, length of exposure is an important coefficient when it comes to any of these vectors. Minimizing the potential exposure time is something that you should always aim for; the best mushroom cultivators work quickly and smoothly, exhibiting the sort of swift activity that you'll see in the best labs. Keep jars or agar plates open for the smallest amount of time possible; inoculate quickly, sterilize often, and don't take too long doing anything. You'll get better at this as you go along, but remember that the less time contaminants have to get in, the less likely they are to get a foot in the door and ruin your substrate.

When mold is this bad, dispose of the whole jar. Don't risk opening it.

This grain looks a little damp, but for now, it's fine.

Grain

It's easy to get complacent when growing on grain, as it seems more hardy and therefore less vulnerable to mold and other issues than brown rice substrate and the like. This isn't the case. We've experienced mold on popcorn, birdseed and a bunch of other bulk substrates, even when we've followed what we thought were fairly standard sterile procedures. Wet spot is commonly found in grain jars, as is pink mold (*Neurospora*), which is an incredibly fast-growing mold that can take over entire jars before you've even noticed; it can colonize an agar plate in 24 hours. Pink mold grows through filter discs, meaning it can very easily spread to other grain jars if it's present on one; as ever, remove and destroy all affected materials if you see pink mold present.

Blue-green mold (*Penicillium spp.*) also likes grain, as does black mold, so you should check the jars regularly for any sign of growth that's not stringy and white, as your mycelial growth should be.

When performing grain-to-grain transfers, you should also do so inside a glove box that's recently been cleaned, and you should keep the jars open for as short an amount of time as you can. Glove boxes are not entirely sterile, so the less air the jars are exposed to, the better.

The blue on the inside of dried PF Tek cakes is not mold, but bruising.

Stunted Growth in Grain Jars

Sometimes after inoculation you'll find that your grain jars aren't exhibiting any mycelial growth. This could be happening for a number of reasons.

The first is lack of heat. We've spoken about this in earlier chapters, but adequate heat is essential to any mushroom grow, and if you're trying to cultivate in the wrong season, it's just not going to happen. You can, of course, create a warmer, more humid environment through heaters and humidifiers, but this will drive up your utility bill and can introduce a whole range of problems. As ever, it's better to go along with nature and grow in the warmer months of the year. Unless you're going through an industrial amount of mushrooms per week, you should be able to grow enough in the summer to get through the winter.

Lack of humidity is another potential issue that can affect mushroom growth. If there's not enough air moisture, you might not see the rate of growth that you want. If you are experiencing low humidity, you might want to invest in building a fruiting chamber, as shown in Chapter 5.

Your grow could be suffering from a lack of oxygen / gas exchange. If the holes in your lids aren't large enough, there won't be fresh air coming into the lids and stale air going out. A quick fix for stunted growth in jars is to simply invert them at around 80% colonization, for the rest of the incubation stage. This allows any build-up of CO_2 to drain out more easily and should kick-start your growth. It's important to keep the jars inverted until fully colonized—any disturbances can mix your dry vermiculite barrier into contact with uncolonized substrate, increasing the contamination risk. It's not something you want to do immediately, as the uncolonized substrate is more vulnerable. If your jars are less than around 80% colonized, just wait it out. Also, you can check your rate of growth every few days by using a fine marker to trace the leading edge of the mycelium onto the glass. If you do this regularly (say every two days) and measure the distance between each line you can identify slow-growing mycelium by the lines getting closer together. By keeping track of growth this way, you can reliably tell if your growth is slowing down, or if you're just getting impatient (we know the feeling!).

Excessive dryness can stunt growth in a pretty serious way. If you didn't introduce the right amount of water to your substrate, the mycelium simply won't grow. In grain jars, you might experience a fair amount of growth that then slows or stops; in this situation, you can perform a grain-to-grain transfer, using your overly dry but still somewhat colonized grain to inoculate a grain jar or bag that's been properly soaked. This should kick-start the mycelium back into proper growth; after all, they only want a little more water! As ever, do this grain-to-grain transfer in a glove box or still air environment, as shown in Chapter 9. However, apply some common sense to issues like this; if you have spare liquid culture or spore suspension, it may be easier to simply start again with your ready-prepared grain. Injecting viable spores or liquid culture poses a much lower contamination risk than transferring partially colonized grain. Though you might be semi-certain that your problem is a lack of moisture, it could just as eas-

Ensure your shrooms are thoroughly dried, so they won't mold in storage.

ily be caused by other problems such as contamination or a poor strain. When you think you've identified a solution, it's always worth stopping to ask yourself how certain you are—if in doubt, just start again.

Bacterial contamination is the end of your grain jar, if you're unlucky enough to experience it. If the growth is patchy and inconsistent and seems to stop in some places, you may have a bacterial contamination. Don't panic; most growth is somewhat patchy to begin with, but if the rest of the growth is fairly even and there are noticeable patches where mycelium have stalled out, you may have to sacrifice that jar to the god of Not Ruining the Whole Rest of Your Grow.

To Breed or Not to Breed

If this was a cannabis grow book, we'd have spent at least a quarter of our time talking about breeding. Usually, when a grower has got their cultivation and consistency on point, they start to look at how to improve the genetics that they're working with and how to do this themselves via selective breeding for a certain trait.

Unfortunately, this isn't quite as easy to do for the mushroom homegrower.

In the cannabis world, time has been taken to develop very distinct and stable strains within the three species; these species are *Cannabis sativa*, *Cannabis indica* and *Cannabis ruderalis*. Hundreds of different strains exist

Believe it or not, this is a veil, not a cobweb.

within these species; for instance, within the *Cannabis sativa* species, there are sativa strains such as Durban Poison, Sour Diesel and Original Haze. These strains exhibit very distinct growth and flowering patterns, different maturation times, different resistance to pests and environmental factors and very different tastes, smells and potencies.

When people think of breeding mushrooms, they often think of the situation in the context above. In the mushroom world, however, "strains" like this simply don't exist, or at best are extremely hard to define. The different types of mushrooms we discussed in Chapter 1 are distinct species; *P. cubensis* is a different species from *P. azurescens*, and both are different

Trichoderma *has taken over this improperly pasteurized grain.*

species than *P. baeocystis*. While they are separate species, they simply don't enjoy the obvious variation in traits that cannabis species and strains do. Any claims of differences in potency between mushroom strains are difficult to verify empirically, due to the incredibly subjective nature of psychedelics and people's experience with them. Added to this is the fact that environmental and methodological variations will also complicate matters. The exact same batch of shrooms might seem much stronger to a person who hasn't eaten much on a given day; the same batch of shrooms might seem a lot milder if a person eats the dried fruit instead of grinding the shrooms into a powder and ingesting them in capsules. It's nearly impossible to objectively define the strength of mushrooms without a chemistry lab, and for this reason any claims about potency really have to be taken with an entire vat of salt.

The same applies for traits like growing speed, yield and size. Environmental factors will be so incredibly varied that you would need highly controlled (preferably lab grade) growing conditions in order to check that you're observing the real effects of a strain rather than the effects of variations in temperature, moisture, nutrient content and the presence of contaminants. Some cannabis strains can take up to 15 weeks to finish while others take only six; when cultivating mushrooms, the timeframe is much narrower, even with different species.

You might have seen head shops selling spores for particular strains of mushrooms, usually purporting to be some new or fascinating strain of *P. cubensis*. Usually, this is simply the vendors trying to apply the cannabis-market methodology to the mushroom-cultivation business, and in some cases succeeding (*a fool and his money are soon parted* after all). There's a lot of argument in the shroom community (or the shroomunity, if you will) over one particular phrase that you might have heard already: "A cube is a cube." This refers to the claim that although individual strains may differ from one another, *P. cubensis* is essentially always the same in terms of characteristics. Of course, this is something of a controversial statement—if you want to stir up an argument in a chat room, simply typing "Ecuadorians are the strongest mushrooms" is a great way to start a fight. Certain strains such as the fabled Pink Buffalo are, to some, worthy of note, while others consider it just another variety of *P. cubensis*. Our view is that they'll

This mushroom has made it! Good work, mushroom.

all get you high in the end. Getting into mushroom strains is like a gardener getting into heirloom vegetables—they have interesting cultural histories and slight differences in taste, but once you eat them they're just the same chemicals in the end.

It's easy to convince unaware and inexperienced mushroom growers that you've got the magical spores that they need, but we believe that psilocybin mushroom species are simply too similar to warrant cross-breeding between species. It's theoretically possible to create such hybrids, but to our knowledge it's never been documented and is incredibly difficult to do in practice, as every combination needs to be grown to fruiting stage, and its spores tested for viability, before a new species can be declared. Plus the legal issues means you'd have problems publishing your findings in any reputable journal!

If you do accidentally or purposely grow something cool, interesting or

The fluff around the base of these shrooms is tomentose mycelium, not mold.

otherwise out of the ordinary, you can clone it fairly easily using the methods shown in Chapter 10. We'd be thrilled to hear of someone finding a cool mutant strain of some sort and cloning it successfully. However, you shouldn't make this your primary concern. If you want to experiment with other species, there are many to try, some more challenging than others.

In conclusion, from a functional perspective, we don't really see the point of strain optimization for the home mushroom-grower. It would be much easier and more worthwhile to spend time and money on optimizing other variables of your grow, such as temperature and moisture. That's not to say that there's no merit in the practice of selective mushroom breeding, but given the illegal status of psilocybin-containing materials in much of the world, it's difficult to determine anything empirically. Of course, if you do want to explore the breeding side of mushroom cultivation, there are a number of resources open to you. We'd recommend The Shroomery in particular for this. Good luck!

Growing Shrooms in Hydrogen Peroxide

Growing mushrooms in hydrogen peroxide is a relatively new concept. To our knowledge, it was R. Rush Wayne who popularized the idea in his 2001 publication *Growing Mushrooms the Easy Way: Home Mushroom Cultivation with Hydrogen Peroxide.* Wayne was supposedly discouraged from the idea of home cultivation by the list of equipment needed and the idea of trying to keep a sterile environment for much of the grow in an otherwise fairly unsterile household. He got the idea for using hydrogen peroxide after reading that orchid growers added it to the culture medium to kill yeast, bacteria and fungus while allowing the orchid seeds to remain viable thanks to their peroxide-decomposing enzymes.

This sort of self-sterilization sounds like a bit of a dream solution to wannabe shroom growers who can't seem to keep growing-environments free of contaminants; the theory goes that nothing would really be able to grow on a hydrogen peroxide–treated shroom medium other than the shrooms themselves. In reality, we haven't found this to be the case.

We actually set out in this book to include hydrogen peroxide as an alternative PF Tek method. We liked the idea, and if it proved to be a simpler method for beginner growers, we wanted to be able to offer it to those who might struggle to sterilize their grow space.

However, we have never found this method to be successful—even with

We've found that growing on hydrogen peroxide does not provide a sterile medium.

This is what happened when we grew with hydrogen peroxide. Not good.

our somewhat overzealous sterilization (one of us is a scientist, after all). As well as not seeming to grow much, our hydrogen peroxide jars all succumbed to mold, and in a pretty serious way. It was quite the impressive collection of colors and types of contamination! We also think that it's probably harder for most home growers to get hold of an adequate type and amount of hydrogen peroxide than it is for them to get all the equipment necessary for basic PF Tek.

By all means, have a go at this method. You can find it outlined in full in the aforementioned book. With the comments above, we simply mean to honestly describe our experience with the method. We don't at all mean to undermine the efforts of R. Rush Wayne; we fully support any method to further the science of psilocybin growing and we especially support any efforts to make it easier for the home grower. There's every chance that Mr. Wayne simply had tapped into a process that we failed to recreate; however, a true scientific contribution requires reproduction of results by independent observers, and this was clearly not the case for us. There are some merits in applying it to patches of mold on the surface of your bulk substrates / casings, but we wouldn't really consider this revolutionary. Considering pressure cookers are cheap, reusable and widely available, we don't see how hydrogen peroxide would be a viable alternative, even if it were as reliable.

Chapter 12

Drying Mushrooms and Storing Spores

So you've got your hefty batch of freshly picked mushrooms. You can't stop looking at them (it's okay, we understand that feeling). But you didn't grow them for their aesthetic qualities; let's get on with drying and consuming them!

Many people consume their mushrooms the easy way; by drying them out over a few days and then simply eating them. This is a perfectly valid consumption method and one that we've all done. However, there are a number of other, more practical and much more delicious ways to enjoy your psilocybin mushrooms.

You can, in fact, eat your freshly harvested shrooms without drying them. You can eat them as soon as they're picked and clean of any remnants of the substrate; obviously if you've grown on manure, you'll want to make this process as thorough as it can be. Fresh shrooms have a slightly sweet taste and are, for the most part, just like any other type of fresh mushroom you'd eat. It's claimed that fresh shrooms are more potent than dried, although this is one of those things that's always difficult to prove. There could be some truth in this, and it relates to the presence and stability of the two active compounds in psychedelic mushrooms: psilocin and psilocybin.

273

A pile of freshly picked shrooms ready to be dried!

Psilocin is thought to be in higher concentration in fresh mushrooms than in dried, as it is an unstable compound that is rapidly broken down by light and oxygen. Psilocybin, however, is far more stable and is turned into the active psilocin in the body. As a result, fresh mushrooms may contain relatively higher concentrations of psilocin, whereas dried may contain mostly psilocybin. Either way, psilocybin is the dominant compound in fresh mushrooms—existing at a concentration around 10 times greater than psilocin. The situation is also muddied somewhat by the fact that because mushrooms lose 90% of their weight when dried, you do have to eat a larger physical amount of fresh shrooms. For instance, if you were planning on consuming a 2-gram dose of dried mushrooms, you would need to consume a 20-gram dose of fresh shrooms in order to get the same effect. This is because all the water weight is still present in the fresh shrooms, and you'll be consuming the water along with all the desired psychoactive compounds.

It is, however, difficult to store fresh shrooms. They'll survive up to five days in the fridge but beyond that will start to rot and turn gross. You can put them in the freezer, where they will store well for a long time, but defrosting them turns them into an icky, gooey mess that's not in the least bit appetizing. As most people can't consume their whole crop of fresh

The caps of these just-picked shrooms are absolutely beautiful.

shrooms in a few days (although many have tried, with hilarious results), it becomes necessary to dry them in order to store them.

After that, there are many methods available to make them less disgusting to consume—because as anyone knows, chewing on dried cubes is never enjoyable. Some of us just truly don't like eating dried mushrooms and will do it if we have to (well, you never *have* to, but you know what we mean), but we'd rather not spend 10 minutes choking them down while trying not to retch everything up like a cat with a magical hairball. If gnawing on bits of fungus makes you feel physically sick, or you value the input of your taste buds over your desire to get a little psychologically funky, it doesn't take a lot of time or effort to turn your crop into something that's close to delicious, so we highly recommend

This stem is hollow inside, as the mushroom has lost 90% of its weight while drying.

275

A well-dried mushroom with a crispy cap.

having a go at some of these other methods of consumption. They each have their own benefits and downfalls, but each one works. Trust us; we've tried.

Before all this, though, you should consider making spore prints from your own freshly picked shrooms. This will allow you to start your next grow without purchasing spores from a third party. In fact, if you get used to making spore prints from at least one mushroom from every grow, you'll have the simplest method to ensure self-sufficiency for as long as you're growing.

Spore Prints

When your mushrooms start look ready, you should start thinking about making a spore print. This is how you collect spores for inoculation of a new substrate, effectively keeping the cycle of mushroom cultivation going with absolutely no extra cost and very little effort.

We've talked in previous chapters about cloning and how successful and reliable this can be. However, cloning as a regular method of substrate inoculation has its downsides. When you clone a mushroom, you are effectively working with an aging cell line, and when you clone that same cell line again

276

Making your own spore prints provides the source of your next grow.

and again, the cell line continues to age. As with anything (as we all, unfortunately, know from experience), with age comes a whole host of downsides; your mushrooms may experience slowed growth, lack of vigor, malformation and smaller yields. This slow genetic demise is known as senescence, and it will negatively affect your mushroom cultivation in the long run.

However, when new spores are germinated, a new "strain" with different genetic variation is created. Making spore prints can help you escape encroaching senescence in your grow. If, after cloning, you find that your growth is a bit laggy and your yields are suffering, introducing some new germinated spores will ensure more vigorous growth and will bring a bit of life back to your grow op. If you're looking to expand or diversify your strain collection within your culture, collecting and germinating new spores is the way to go.

The gills of the mushroom drop spores, ensuring a new generation of shrooms.

Thankfully, making a spore print is easy as pie. You will need to keep an eye on your mushrooms and pick a couple of the strongest-looking ones as potentials for spore prints. You'll need to pick your mushrooms BEFORE they drop their spores; afterwards, they're no good for this process. When it comes time to create your spore print, pick the best-looking mushroom that still hasn't

277

dropped. One spore print will be enough; a print contains thousands of spores (a single mushroom produces hundreds of thousands of spores) and all you need is a couple of viable ones to ensure your next grow.

You can create spore prints on bits of paper, plates of glass or pieces of foil. We like foil, as it's disposable, cheap and easy to work with, but that's just our preference. However, foil and glass allow for presterilization; this isn't possible when making prints on paper, meaning that contaminants may be present. For this reason, we wouldn't recommend using paper. Using foil also makes it easy to mail spore prints to other cultivators, and storage of them inside your own home is simple and doesn't take up much space. In fact, using the method outlined below, spore prints can be stored for years in the right conditions.

Use a Glove Box

We've created a spore print outside of a glove box so you can see exactly what we're doing, but you should always perform this inside a glove box. Also ensure that you flame-sterilize your scalpel before use.

Besides your mushroom, you'll need a sharp scalpel, a small piece of foil and a sterile jar in which to keep your print.

Ensure that you store your spore print at room temperature and in a safe, dry place. They will remain viable for years when stored like this. Proper labeling is essential for good record-keeping.

To do this, you'll take your sterile spore print and a small volume of sterile, distilled water (to fill a 10 ml syringe), and will simply use a scalpel to scrape a few spores from the print into the water. You can also scrape the entire spore print into a larger volume of sterile liquid and use this to fill a number of syringes for later use; for instance, you could use 50 ml of water and make five spore syringes to keep you going for a few applications. Do whatever suits you best.

Let the syringes sit for 24 hours before inoculating with them, as the spores need to rehydrate before they can be used. It's best to keep your spore syringes in your fridge if you can; they will keep at room temperature but a fridge is always preferable. They will stay viable for years when kept in the fridge.

If you haven't been too careful with your spores, or have received a sample you don't trust to be sterile, agar can help you check for contamination. See Chapter 10 for more detail on this.

Making Spore Prints

1. Grab a scalpel, a jar, a piece of foil and some ready-to-pick shrooms.

2. Pick a mushroom that hasn't dropped its spores and twist it off the cake.

3. Flame-sterilize your scalpel then cut the mushroom just below the cap.

4. Remove the lid from your jar. Place a square of foil inside the jar.

5. Gently place the cap, gills down, onto the foil square.

6. Make sure it's centered and that none of the cap is overhanging the foil. *Continues* →

7. Close the lid of the jar tightly before any dirt gets inside.

8. Leave the jar for 24 hours. Make sure it isn't knocked or moved.

9. After 24 hours, the spores should have dropped onto the foil. Like this!

10. Gently place the spore print into your hand, print-side up.

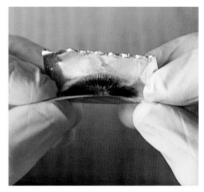

11. Fold the print in half, with the print staying inwards.

12. Fold the edges inwards. You can use the scalpel to help you.

13. Use a marker to label the folded foil containing the spore print.

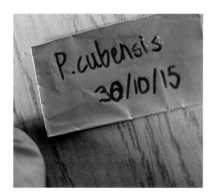

14. Note the species and the date that the print was made.

15. Store the print in a safe, dry place and it will stay viable for years.

Keep your stash out of sight and in a secure place.

Basic Drying

Once you've got a nice crop of fresh shrooms, the first thing to do is to dry them. You'll read a lot of stuff online about ideal temperatures and humidity levels as well as some Rube Goldberg–machine set ups that are incredibly over-engineered for their purpose, but realistically, all this is unnecessary. Forums are teeming with talk of the need for speed, with spurious claims that if you leave the mushrooms to dry out on their own, they will begin to rot. In our experience, this has never happened and we've never been in a rush to get our shrooms dry. You'll also read talk of the need to fan dry or to place the mushrooms on bits of kitchen paper or other porous materials. Again, we've never found this to be the case.

The goal of drying your mushrooms is to rid them of any water content and thus preserve for long-term storage. While fresh shrooms will last up to five days in the fridge, dried shrooms will last a hell of a long time when stored properly. We've had three-year-old samples that have shown no noticeable drop in potency! As mushrooms are up to 90% water, they'll reduce to 10% of their wet weight when dried, so you can use this fact as one good way to test dryness. Weigh your shrooms before drying, then divide that number by 10—this is your rough target dry weight. A few percent either side of this should be fine.

Aren't they beautiful? Dried shrooms are like a work of art.

Drying Your Mushrooms

1. Lay your freshly picked mushrooms on something like a sushi-rolling mat.

2. The gaps in the mat allow for airflow, ensuring even drying.

3. Leave the mat in a safe, dry place, like an airing cupboard or boiler room.

4. Check the mushrooms daily. Be on the lookout for mold or any lingering dampness.

5. As they dry, the shrooms will shrink. This is normal!

6. After seven days, take a mushroom and try to bend its stem between your fingers.

7. If it bends but doesn't break, like this, it's still too wet.

8. You can also bend the cap to check. Be gentle!

9. This mushroom still isn't completely dry. Put it back for another day.

10. The clean break in this cap means it is dry. Hooray!

If you have an airing cupboard or boiler room, this will be the ideal space in which to dry your crop. However, you can really dry them in any space where they're not likely to be knocked over or disturbed; the higher, the better (if you'll pardon the pun). We've found that sushi-rolling mats are great for this purpose, as they allow some airflow through the holes in the mat. Ensure that none of your shrooms are touching, then leave them. Check back every day; they are ready when they are cracker dry—this means you should be able to snap them in half cleanly, without the stems bending. This should take up to five days, but it may not be completely achievable if your household relative humidity is high and / or your temperature is low. If they're almost dry but still slightly bendy, you can finish the job by putting them into a jar or other airtight container with some desiccant to pull out any remaining moisture that may make your shrooms go bad. You can buy packets of desiccant online; these are the types of packets filled with silica gel that you get in clothes pockets or camera bags. However, rice and cat litter are also great desiccants, too. Ensure that the cat litter says "100% silica gel crystals" under ingredients and avoid anything that's perfumed, and it should be all good. We like to wrap a handful of this litter in a sheet of Tyvek, tie it with an elastic band and drop it into the jar containing our shrooms.

The blue tint on this mushroom is bruising. This is totally natural.

Store your dried shrooms in a jar with a bag or packet of desiccant.

You can, of course, use a dehydrator if you have one, but we've never had any problems with the method above and don't really see why you would need to make it any more complicated than that. There are a few situations in which a dehydrator might be necessary, for instance if you experience high relative humidity all year round (if you live in the tropics, for example) or you have some industrial-size batches of fresh shrooms, in which case investing in a dehydrator is probably a good idea. Shrooms usually take around 24 hours to dry in a dehydrator. You should aim for a drying temperature of around 120°F (49°C). Basically, we say keep it simple. Life's difficult, man; take it easy when you can!

When your mushrooms are dried fully, it's time to start thinking about how to consume them. As mentioned, you can simply eat them if you like. Most people do. However, they tend to be gross, and it can be a bit haphazard to properly dose yourself this way. There are better ways to consume your dried mushrooms.

Chapter 13

Consuming Your Shrooms

Environment and company are essential to having a good trip. Make sure you're in a safe, comfortable, relaxing place with people that you trust and enjoy; and if it's your first time, try to ensure that you're with a good friend who has taken shrooms before. Get some good music, movies, games or whatever you like to do and settle in to see how it goes. At first, you'll likely find that things start to look a little odd; walls might appear to breathe, colors might be more intense, and everything that you say might suddenly be hilarious. The beauty of shrooms is their ability to turn everything on its head. Light and sounds will be fascinating, and you'll no doubt end up chatting about everything from your feelings to the state of the universe. It's a fantastic place to be. Enjoy it!

A potential bummer whilst on shrooms is getting stuck in a negative cycle of thoughts. You can experience anxiety, and then you can become anxious about your anxiety, leading to a bit of a sticking thought pattern. However, if you stay alert and aware of your own feelings, you'll be able to easily let go of any negative thoughts and drive yourself into a more positive way of thinking. Tell your friends that you're feeling a bit blue and let them bring you into a better place. You're only journeying through your own mind; there's nothing in there that can hurt you.

If all else fails, remember: mushrooms can't really hurt you, and eventually it will pass. And next time, take less.

What to Do If You're Feeling Too High

If you feel that you've gotten a little too high, let someone you trust know. Do whatever you think would make you feel more comfortable; that could be burying yourself in a duvet and watching the pretty lights on the TV, or cuddling, or walking around your garden and looking at the stars. Stay

Eating dried shrooms will produce a come-up time of 45–60 minutes.

🍄 A Note on Dosing

When it comes to getting the right dose of shrooms, it's almost completely subjective. One person's screamingly high dose is another person's mild buzz-inducing dose. The only real way to figure out a good dose for you is through trial and error, and for this reason we always, always recommend underdosing rather than overdosing. If you've never ever taken shrooms before, start with half a gram of dried or 5 grams of fresh. Mushrooms can take up to an hour to kick in, depending on how you take them, so wait and see how you feel after about an hour or 90 minutes, and then take more if you feel that you want to. Repeat until you don't want to get any higher. Your trip will likely last around four to six hours, with a peak a couple of hours in.

Capsules allow for accurate dosing and easy transportation.

with your friend or partner, eat if you feel like eating, and just take deep breaths; you just have to wait until the intensity passes. Don't try and fight any uncomfortable sensations or thoughts, simply experience them, let them pass and remember the effects will wear off. Yoga breathing is incredibly helpful in these situations.

The more experienced amongst you might be taking doses of 3.5 to 5 dry grams or more, depending on just how mentally funky you like to get. In that case, you probably know what you're doing, so we'll trust you to dose yourself accordingly. However, keep in mind this isn't high school and you don't have to prove how much you can handle. How much you choose to take matters little; super high doses don't make you Timothy Leary, and gentle low doses don't make you Nancy Reagan. Some people will mock those who prefer low doses. We like to call these people "assholes."

All the recipes in this book are based on a low dose of 0.5 dry grams, in order to allow you to take as much or as little as you want. We are pretty experienced psychonauts and we still find that from time to time we'll be pushing open the doors of perception at one gram or less. Many things can affect your tolerance to mushrooms: how much you've slept / eaten / drunk that day, whether or not you're ill, what form you're consuming them in, etc. For this reason, we always dose low and take more if necessary. However, if you're making some of the chocolate found later in this chapter, or the shakes, or whatever, feel free to increase the dose per chocolate / shake / whatever. If you do make a few of these recipes

Powdering dried mushrooms is easy and helps to digest them.

at once, it's best to keep a consistent dose in everything to avoid confusion later on. We trust you!

Eating Your Mushrooms

You can eat your shrooms. Fresh or dried, it doesn't matter; a 10-gram dose of fresh shrooms is equivalent to a 1-gram dose of dried shrooms. This is the most common way to consume mushrooms, and it's perfectly acceptable. Shrooms don't taste great, but they're not the worst things in the world, and eating the dried shrooms will produce a reliable come-up time of between 45 and 60 minutes. You can shorten this onset considerably if you have an empty stomach. Eat more if you want them. Stop when you're high enough. It's very simple.

Basic Tea

The second most popular way of consuming shrooms is to make a tea, which can be done with either fresh or dried shrooms. This is a very simple method that allows for quick uptake, although it's not the most pleasant tasting. It's fairly easy to dose with this method, although there can be some slight variation between doses, and sometimes you can come up *too* quickly. To avoid this, sip the tea; don't throw it down your throat.

If you're using dried, you might want to first grind your mushrooms to a powder, which can be done using a coffee or spice grinder. You can use your normal coffee grinder (as long as you clean it thoroughly afterwards, or your morning cup is going to get a lot more interesting) but we prefer to have a dedicated grinder for shrooms, so there's no cross-contamination of flavors (or psychedelic material). You can make tea with whole shrooms, in which case just finely chop them up.

Basic Tea Recipe

Makes 2 teas

(1 tea = 0.5 gram dose)

- 10 grams wet (fresh) or 1 gram dried mushrooms
- 2 cups boiling water
- 2 or 3 green tea bags (or whatever tea you choose)
- Juice of ½ lemon
- 1 tbsp. honey

Making Basic Mushroom Tea

1. Grab all of your ingredients. If you're vegan, use agave instead of honey.

2. Chop up your fresh shrooms. Be careful with that knife!

3. Remember that 10 grams of fresh shrooms are equal to 1 gram of dry.

4. Place the boiling water in a jug and add in the mushrooms.

5. Stir them a little; ensure that they're submerged.

6. Add in the teabags and stir again to submerge them.

7. Add in the lemon juice and let the tea steep for 15 minutes.

8. Using a sieve, divide the tea between two cups.

9. Dispose of the mushrooms or keep them for a second less-potent brew.

10. Add your honey or agave and drink! Remember to sip, not gulp.

There are a number of different ways to make your mushroom tea a bit more palatable. Adding sugar is a simple one; stir in the sugar just after you remove the water from the heat. You can also add an actual tea bag to the mushroom mixture, so that it will mask the fungi flavor somewhat; chai, black, licorice and green teas are popular amongst our fellow shroomers. Our preference, however, is for fresh ginger and honey; the ginger helps to relieve any nausea while you're coming up and the honey makes the mixture a little nicer to the taste buds. Experiment and find what works best for you.

Lemon Tek

Possibly the simplest consumption method with the most immediate and most intense effects, lemon tek involves soaking your ground mushrooms in lemon juice for half an hour then taking the resulting lemon juice like a shot. Some people swear by this method, claiming it brings the high on incredibly quickly.

The theory behind this method is that instead of waiting for the acids in your stomach to break down the mushrooms, you're creating an outside environment for that to happen in; namely, the acid in the lemon juice. Thus the psilocybin starts to break down into psilocin before you've ingested it, allowing your body to just grab hold of that psilocin when you swallow the liquid and send you off on that trip before you know it. It's worth noting that these claims are made by people on the internet, and there is very little evidence that this actually occurs.

You'll need to use the juice of a lemon; make sure that the liquid completely covers your ground-up shrooms. If you choose to leave the solution for longer than 30 minutes, then there may be a more advanced breakdown of psilocybin and you'll likely get higher quicker. However, we think that 30 minutes is about right.

Use real lemon juice for this method, not the stuff out of a bottle. You don't have to add a teaspoon of honey before you take the shot, but it makes it a little more palatable and the sugar can help take the edge off the trip a little bit. However, feel free to leave this out if you prefer. Some have said that adding a shot of whiskey or rum to the mixture is also a good way to mask the taste, but we'd never recommend that of course.

Dosing in this method can be difficult, as the experience is so intense.

Lemon Tek

1. Grab your ground mushroom powder and the fresh juice of a lemon.

2. Pour the mushroom powder into the lemon juice.

3. Stir it until it's well combined. It will look gross.

4. Pour the whole shebang into a shot glass, because you're fancy.

5. Let it settle. There's no improving on this presentation.

6. Knock it back like a champ. Sorry it tastes so bad.

For a trip that comes on quickly but is relatively mild, consider a micro-dose of 0.3 grams. That should leave you nicely funky without wiping you out entirely. Don't worry if you don't have the scales to weigh out a dose this low, simply weigh out a gram and split it three ways. A normal dose for one person with lemon tek is between .5 and 1 gram per person. Always dose lower than you first think; remember, you can always take more.

Lemon Tek Recipe

Makes 1 shot

(1 shot = 0.5 gram – 1 gram dose)

- 0.5 – 1 gram dried mushrooms, ground to a powder
- The juice of 1 lemon

Making Capsules

If you can't be bothered to try any of the recipes or other advanced consumption methods in this book, then the single best thing that you can do is invest in a cheap capsule-making kit and start making your own mushroom capsules. It's incredibly easy but has an incredible amount of benefits. You can buy these kits from any sort of online head shop or even on some larger retail sites, and if you're uncomfortable buying things online they can be fairly easily sourced in real life. All you'll need to make the dried mushrooms into powder form is a regular coffee grinder, though it's preferable here to use an old one or have one that's only used for this purpose.

One of the benefits of making capsules is that you can be sure of getting an exact dose every time (or as close as possible), and it can be a lot easier to manage your consumption when things are in capsules as opposed to in tea or in mushroom form. Because they're in powder form, the onset should be faster, and you avoid all the grossness of the taste. If you're vegan or vegetarian, it's easy to find capsules that suit your dietary requirement at health food stores or online. Capsules are also easy to transport without worrying about people finding your shrooms. Keep them in a prescription medicine or nutritional supplement container and they'll appear to be any normal type of medication. This is definitely more stealthy than carrying around baggies of dried shrooms on a night out or a wander in the forest.

Making Mushroom Capsules

1. Weigh out enough dried shrooms for .5 of a gram per capsule, according to how many capsules you are making.

2. Place the mushrooms into an old coffee grinder or a small blender.

3. Pulse the grinder to break up the mushrooms.

4. They'll eventually become a fine powder, like this.

5. Push one half of the capsule into every hole in the capsule maker. Top and bottom!

6. These are vegetarian-friendly capsules, size 00. These should hold half a gram each.

7. Place the capules in the holes according to the instructions on your kit.

Continues →

8. Shake some of the mushroom powder out onto the bottom section of the maker.

9. Push the powder around to get it to fall into the capsules. You can use a credit card.

10. Use this tool from your kit to push the powder into the capsules.

11. Push down with equal force, but not too hard. We don't want to break anything.

12. Some of the powder will now be packed down into the capsule halves.

13. Move the remaining powder around, letting it fall into the holes again.

14. Cutting the powder helps, as if … well, you get the idea.

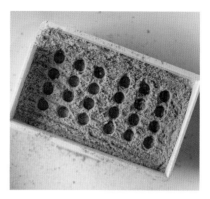

15. Push again with the pushing tool, filling the capsules further.

16. Add the remaining powder so that none is left over.

17. Keep repeating this, even when it seems that the capsules are full.

18. You'll get there eventually; don't get frustrated and waste any powder!

19. A chopping motion helps to get those last little bits inside.

Continues →

20. Push any excess powder off the corner and out of the way.

21. Take the upper part of the capsule maker and line it up with the bottom.

22. Press it into place, putting the top and bottom halves of the capsules together.

23. Push down with even force, as according to the instructions on your maker.

24. Gently turn the whole thing over, being very careful.

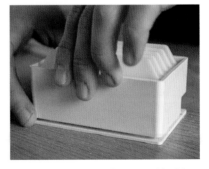

25. Settle it upside down and hold the bottom down with your fingers.

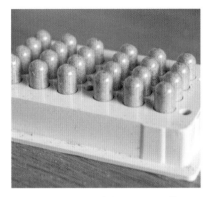

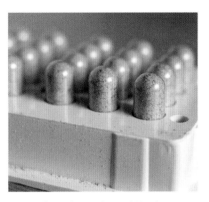

26. Ease the top of the maker off to reveal your perfectly made capsules.

27. Look at those things! Each one has a .5 gram dose.

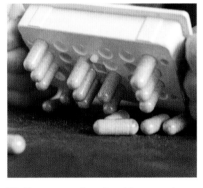

28. Turn the maker upside down once again and push on the back gently.

29. Your capsules should pop out fully formed, just like this.

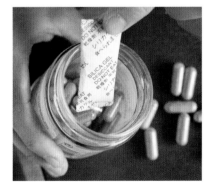

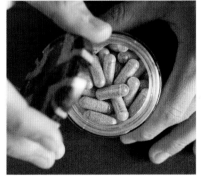

30. Keep the capsules in a glass jar with some silicia gel desiccant.

31. Secure the lid and keep them in a safe place, away from medications.

The downside to putting your mushrooms into capsules is that it can look a bit more sketchy, as you can't tell if pills contain just shrooms or other substances. This is especially important for psychedelics where your starting mindset plays a huge role in the chances of you enjoying the experience. Only share with friends who you trust, and who trust you. And, in fact, you shouldn't take mushroom capsules when offered to you unless you trust the person and know them well; one powder can be easily exchanged for another and you could end up taking an unknown dose of an unknown substance or just bunk filler, instead of the mushrooms that you wanted. Be smart, kids.

Our preferred dose when making shroom capsules is 0.5 g in a 00 capsule. This allows you to get a moderate trip or to double up and get a stronger experience. 26 g will make 52 caps.

If you make a few of these and want to store them for a while, pop a desiccant packet in your container to keep that pesky moisture out.

While we advocate responsible drug use at all times, there is also the possibility of mixing up your mushrooms with other drugs to make your capsules a one-stop-Hippy-Flip-shop. Hippy Flipping is the process of taking MDMA along with mushrooms, and we can tell you from personal experience that if you get the dosing and environment right, it can be a great time. However, we'll leave this up to you—and remember, illegal drugs are illegal.

Basic Alcohol Extraction

Extracting psilocybin into alcohol is both easy and convenient. When it comes time to trip, you'll need only a couple of drops of an alcohol extraction rather than a handful of dried shrooms or a cup of potentially quite disgusting tea. With a well-mixed solution, dosing is consistent and accurate, and you can mix a couple of drops of your extract into any other liquid for ease of consumption. Storage also is incredibly easy; your extraction will be kept in a light-resistant dropper bottle, meaning that it can be kept in your fridge or freezer and out of sight of everybody else. Kept in the freezer, it will remain viable for years.

The downsides of this method are that the shelf life is relatively hard to predict when kept at room temperature, and even when kept in the fridge or freezer for longer periods of time. Some might find the technique a little too time consuming for them, though we haven't found this to be the case. The main drawback to this method, however, is that—as with all liquid extractions—it can be very easy to get carried away and overdose yourself. Instead of a few drops, you do several more, and then you're higher than you ever intended to be. Maintain a low-dosing technique with alcohol extractions; remember, you can always take more.

Despite the simplicity of this method, it has to be completed over a few days. This shouldn't be an issue; it's a do-and-leave sort of technique. You'll need to have purchased a dark-glass 1 fluid ounce dropper bottle, which are widely available online, and you'll also need a coffee filter and a clean syringe. Your alcohol should be ethanol of between 75% and 95% ABV (151–190 proof). Everclear is a commercial alcohol that comes in both 151 and 190 proof versions, and you can absolutely use these types for this extraction, but you can also buy bottles of high-proof ethanol online or from medical supply stores.

 Warning!
Do NOT use methanol for this extraction. Methanol is poisonous to humans. Some techniques online call for you to extract the psilocybin into methanol before evaporating all the methanol and adding ethanol. Just cut out the middleman and use ethanol; far easier, far safer.

For a moderate dose, you'll want to use 10 grams of dried mushrooms per 20 ml of ethanol. We've found this to be a good midpoint, but of course feel free to experiment with stronger or weaker extracts as per your needs. If this is your first alcohol extraction, however, stick to the amounts we've suggested and then find out what strength you prefer through trial and error.

After soaking the mushroom material in the alcohol, our method calls for you to leave the liquid out for the ethanol to evaporate. The extent to which the alcohol evaporates doesn't matter, because you'll measure the amount of liquid you have left and add more ethanol to bring it up to 20 ml; this allows for correct dosing, as the psilocybin content stays the same no matter what the overall volume of the liquid. However, if you leave the ethanol out too long, you might find that you end up with a sticky film on your dish but little else, leaving you panicking that all the solution has evaporated. Don't worry; it hasn't. You can revive your sticky solution by taking 20 ml of ethanol and "washing" the dish with it. This will re-suspend

Basic Alcohol Extraction

1. Ensure you've got everything you'll need, including 75% ethanol or above.

2. Place your dried shrooms into the grinder. We use 10 grams for 20 ml of alcohol.

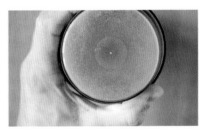

3. Grind the mushrooms into a fine powder. Keep going until it's even.

4. Pour the powder into a recently sterilized glass jar with a lid.

5. Measure out 100 ml of ethanol, or thereabouts.

306

6. Add this ethanol into the jar containing the mushroom powder.

7. Secure the jar lid and tighten it. Make sure it's closed!

8. Give it a good old shake. Go on, you can do better than that!

9. Leave the extract in a dry place overnight.

10. Grab a large bottle, a funnel and a coffee filter. Fold the filter in half.

Continues →

11. Then fold it again, so it's this sort of shape.

12. Open it up to create a cone shape that stays open.

13. Put this coffee filter into the funnel and push it down gently.

14. Wet it a little with water to help it stay in place.

15. Put the funnel into the opening of the bottle and pour in the alcohol.

16. Leave the alcohol to drain until it's done.

17. The extract should look greenish and slightly viscous.

18. The filter should be filled with mushroom matter like this.

19. Squeeze out the last few drops of the extract.

20. Pour into a clean baking dish to evaporate. There should be about 20 mls left after evaporation.

Shots of shroom juice and dried mushrooms aren't exactly delicious, so we've come up with some more-enjoyable ways to consume your psychedelics.

the extract and everything should be fine. We know this works thanks to the inability of one of us to follow basic instructions.

It's also possible to extract psilocybin from dried, used PF Tek cakes using the aforementioned method. When you've harvested your PF Tek cakes, put them in the same place as your harvested mushrooms and let them dry out in the same way. When they appear dry, break them up and allow them to dry even further. They need to be bone dry before you begin. In theory, you can then use the dried cakes in much the same way you've used the mushrooms. However, it can be difficult to know exactly how strong this extraction will be, so exercise caution when dosing. You may want to leave the PF Tek pieces in the alcohol a little longer than normal to extract as much of the remaining psilocybin as possible.

If your cakes exhibit any signs of mold or other contamination, don't use them. Toss them. It's not worth the risk.

Recipes

If, like us, you're pretty at home in the kitchen, there are a whole host of recipes that you can whip up and stuff with your delicious, psychedelic bounty. However, if you're not that handy with a knife or a spatula, we still don't want you to miss out on all the fun! Below are several recipes with varying degrees of difficulty, all designed to enhance your experience with your homegrown shrooms. With all the recipes in this section, one dose is calculated as half a gram; we like to dose low and dose often. Remember: you can always take more, but you can never take less.

Ginger and Lime Chocolates

Who doesn't love chocolate? The ginger in this recipe acts as an antiemetic; that is, it works to counteract the nausea that many people feel when consuming shrooms. The lime juice borrows from the lemon tek recipe above, as the lime juice begins the breakdown of psilocybin to psilocin before it enters your body, making the come-up a little faster. The chocolate is there to make the whole thing taste better, though it's been said that a little dark chocolate can make a trip more intense. This is, of course, near impossible to prove. However, trying never hurts.

Just a brief warning here: these are strong. The lime juice works in the same way as in the lemon tek method above, meaning that there is a fast come-up and the trip seems incredibly intense. We've had doses as low as .75 of a gram before and found that after 15 minutes we were trying to lock ourselves into someone's spare room filled with tiny instruments. Dose low; you can always take more.

Ginger and Lime Chocolates Recipe

Makes 12 chocolates
(1 chocolate = 0.5 gram dose)
- 6 grams dried shrooms
- 50 grams dark chocolate
- 65 grams crystalized ginger
- The zest of ½ a lime
- The juice of ¼ lime

In the forthcoming photo essay we've utilized a silicon chocolate mold we had lying around, because we like things to look pretty and our food to be mainly smooth. However, we're aware that not everyone will have such a mold lying around. For those people, or those who are simply too lazy to dick around with melted chocolate for too long, there's a simpler method later on. Your chocolates will be less attractive, but just as fun.

Ginger and Lime Chocolates – Method 1

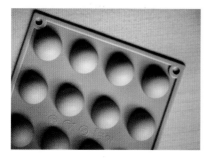

1. Get some good-quality dark chocolate for this. It's worth it.

2. You can use a silicon mold to get good truffle shapes. Or not.

3. Place the dried mushrooms into your old coffee-grinder.

4. Grind the mushrooms to a fine powder. It should look like this.

5. Slowly melt the dark chocolate in a bain-marie or double boiler.

6. In the grinder, blend the crystallized ginger to a near-paste.

7. When the ginger is a paste consistency, add in the lime zest.

8. Then add in the fresh lime juice and blend together in the grinder.

9. Tip the lime-ginger paste out into a bowl.

10. Add in the powdered mushrooms and stir to combine.

11. Don't worry. It will look gross. This is totally normal.

12. With damp hands, squish the mixture together and roll it out on the counter. *Continues* →

313

13. It totally looks like goblin poo. Sorry about this.

14. Roll it out thinly, then cut the poo into four equal sections.

15. Cut the four sections into three pieces, making 12 equal poops.

16. Try to ensure that they are all about the same size.

17. Take the melted chocolate and add a little into each mold.

18. Spread it evenly around the mold to ensure full coverage.

19. Place the mold into the fridge until the chocolate has set.

20. Remove the mold from the fridge and drop a poop ball into each one.

21. Flatten each poop ball. Look, ours fit perfectly!

22. Drop a little melted chocolate onto the top of each poop ball.

Continues →

23. With a spoon or fork, spread the chocolate around.

24. The chocolate should reach over and beyond the edge of each mold.

25. Back in the fridge! Just until the chocolate has set again.

26. Pop the truffles out of the silicon mold. They come out easily.

27. If you like, sprinkle a little cocoa powder for presentation.

Ginger and Lime Chocolates – Method 2

1. If you don't want to make the truffle shapes, there's an easier way!

2. Take each poop ball and flatten it in your hand.

3. Sprinkle some cocoa powder on a piece of foil.

4. Drop the flattened disc into the chocolate and coat it.

5. Turn it over and ensure it's completely covered in chocolate.

6. Place each one onto the foil and sprinkle more cocoa on top.

7. Place into the fridge until the chocolate has set.

8. Voila! Keep them in the fridge until they're to be eaten.

Shroom Jello

Wobbly, hideously artificially flavored, full of sugar and packed with ground mushrooms. What's not to love?

Shroom Jello Recipe

Makes 4 Jell-Os

(1 Jello = 0.5 gram dose)

- 2 grams dried shrooms
- 80 grams Jello powder
- 400 ml water

Making Mushroom Jello

1. Grab your ingredients. We use vegetarian jelly because we're hippies.

2. Put your dried shrooms into your coffee grinder.

3. Grind your shrooms down to a fine powder.

4. Add the jello powder to the water as per packet instructions.

5. Whisk lightly then add in the powdered shrooms.

6. Whisk the whole thing to evenly distribute the powder.

7. Pour out evenly between your molds.

8. Leave to set as per packet instructions, then eat!

9. Ain't nothing like shroom jelly and ice cream!

Salted Chocolate and Ginger Shroom Drops

Sticking to the dark chocolate theme, this recipe is a little easier than the aforementioned chocolate recipe but equally isn't as tasty. The salt and the fresh ginger help to mask the flavor of the mushrooms here, and the ginger helps with nausea.

Salted Chocolate and Ginger Shroom Drops Recipe

Makes 5 drops

(1 drop = 0.5 gram dose)

- 2.5 g dried shrooms
- 50 g dark chocolate
- ½ teaspoon coconut oil
- sea salt
- a small chunk of fresh ginger

Salted Chocolate and Ginger Shroom Drops

1. Get some good dark chocolate for this. It's the best.

2. Slowly melt the chocolate over a bain-marie or double boiler.

3. Add in a little coconut oil if you have it. This is optional.

4. Add in the powdered mushrooms that you've weighed out.

5. Stir to mix the mushrooms into the melted chocolate.

6. Drop five spoonfulls of the chocolate onto some baking paper.

7. Flatten each spoonful of chocolate with the back of a spoon.

8. Grate fresh ginger over the chocolate.

9. Stir the ginger into the chocolate with a knife or fork.

10. Sprinkle the sea salt onto the top of the chocolate.

11. Place the tray into the fridge until the chocolate sets.

12. Remove from the paper and eat, or keep in the fridge.

Shroom Shakes

If you've just recently harvested your PF Tek cakes or your grain and have handfuls of fresh shrooms just begging to be used, then this is a recipe that lets you use those wet mushrooms without drying them. We could get fancy and tell you that we chose blueberries here because of the molecular gastronomy flavor-pairing of mushrooms and blueberries, but suffice it to say that when it came to the choice of fruit here, we gave it some serious thought. As well as all the vitamin C and vitamin K and the other good things inside blueberries, the strong flavor will help to cover the taste of the mushrooms and make the smoothie super delicious. The banana will help settle your stomach here and the honey will sweeten everything up a little. Perfect for a morning pick-me-up-tune-me-in-then-drop-me-out.

Shroom Shakes Recipe

Makes 2 shroom shakes
(1 shake = 0.5 gram dose)
- 10 g wet (fresh) shrooms
- ½ cup blueberries
- 300 ml almond milk (or milk of your choice)
- honey

Making Shroom Shakes

1. Blueberries are best for this recipe, as they actually go with mushrooms.

2. Place the fruit into the container of a hand blender.

3. Add in the fresh shrooms. Honestly, trust us here.

4. Add in whatever sort of milk you're using.

5. Give it all a good blitz with the blender until it's smooth.

6. Slowly pour the smoothie into bottles.

7. Ensure that the smoothies are equally portioned.

8. Voila! Keep in the fridge until use. And sip, don't gulp!

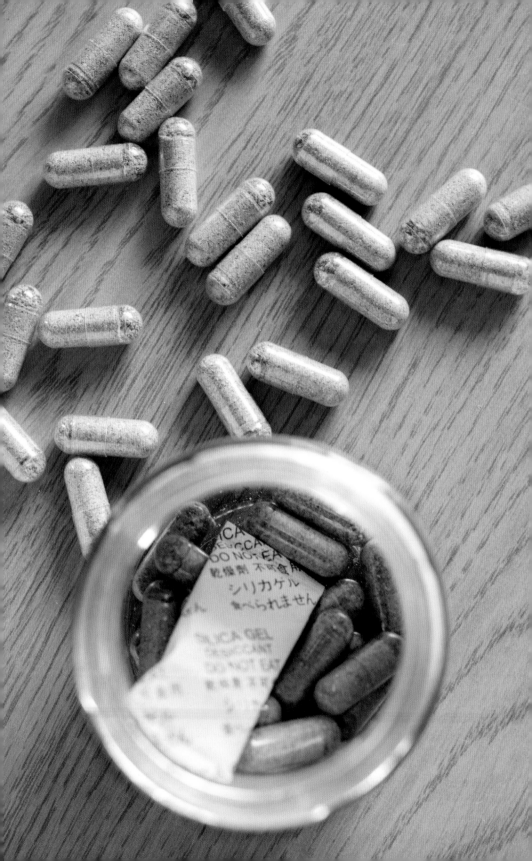

Chapter 14

Microdosing and the Future of Psilocybin as Medicine

In this chapter, we'll be talking about current research into potential medical and psychological uses of psilocybin. As believers in the positive mental effects of psychedelics, we're both interested in and incredibly supportive of such research and we're thrilled that greater exploration into the realm of psychedelics is now being done.

However, while we're going to talk about the perceived positive effects of psilocybin felt by and seen in those suffering from an array of mental health issues, this is in no way a recommendation to begin self-treatment with psilocybin—or any other type of drug.

We're not going to engage in a debate about the forms or ethics of recreational drug use; we're all adults here and all free to make our own educated choices about what to do with our bodies and minds. However, recreational use of intoxicants (and in this we include alcohol, cannabis and psilocybin as well as "harder" drugs) can sometimes become habitual when we are using these things to escape a place in which we feel trapped, physically or mentally. We might begin to lean on our intoxicant of choice as an easy way to make ourselves feel better or to avoid dealing with a problem that's becoming bigger over time. Using any sort of drug in this

Capules can assist in microdosing. Simply fill them with a smaller amount.

way is detrimental to our overall mental health; when problems occur, the only way to diffuse them is to recognize them and to seek help. If you believe that your own use of intoxicants is becoming a negative factor in your life, there are many support groups and organizations available to you.

Many of us will experience mental health issues during our lifetimes. No matter what the degree of severity or length of duration, you should always seek help from trained medical or therapy professionals.

There are a number of organizations that can offer advice if you feel that you are experiencing a mental health issue. In the UK, the Samaritans can be reached 24 hours a day, seven days a week at 0845 790 9090. In the USA, you can reach the Crisis Call Center at 1-800-273-8255. In Canada, the Mental Health Helpline is available at 1-866-531-2600.

One more time: if you are suffering from any sort of mental health issue or believe yourself to be in need of medical assistance, seek real medical help. We very much intend for this chapter to be an educational discussion of how psilocybin may form a part of a cohesive treatment for a number of conditions; we do not intend to imply that anyone should self-medicate— with psilocybin or with anything else.

With that said (and hopefully taken in), there's an incredibly fascinating body of research currently being done into the psychological and medical effects of psilocybin. The potential use of hallucinogens to treat conditions has been known for a long time; between the '50s and the '70s, the U.S. federal government spent $4 million on over 100 studies on LSD and its effects.[12] During that time, it was incredibly easy to obtain psilocybin for research and it, along with other hallucinogens, was tested on a range of subjects, including those suffering from such conditions as obsessive-compulsive disorder, schizophrenia, terminal cancer and alcoholism. When Nixon signed the Controlled Substances Act in 1970, research stalled, and it is only now that we are starting to see a resurgence of the former research.

The Good Friday Experiment

The Good Friday Experiment, conducted by Walter Pahnke under the supervision of Timothy Leary in 1962, can be considered one of the first experiments into the long-term effects of psilocybin on people's spiritual experiences. Based on the use of other substances in some cultures' spiritual practices (e.g., Ayahuasca in the Urarina people of the Peruvian Amazon, or Iboga in the spiritual practice of Bwiti in Gabon, Central Africa), Pahnke reasoned that psilocybin could be used in a religious setting not normally associated with entheogenic use, to enhance the spiritual experience.

Twenty participants were screened and divided into pairs based on their past religious experiences and general psychological profile. At the beginning of the experiment, one member of each pair was randomly assigned to receive either 30 mg psilocybin or an active placebo—nicotinic acid. An active placebo was used to ensure both members felt an initial change in state—nicotinic acid produces skin flushing and a general feeling of relaxation. As all participants had no previous experience with psychedelics, this

Psilocybin mushrooms have been used to treat a variety of conditions.

partially helped to blur the perception of the participants as to which of them had received the psilocybin. However, as the effects of nicotinic acid wore off, it quickly became apparent to all which participants were under the influence of psychedelics!

After this experiment was concluded, all participants were interviewed to understand the nature of their experience at the chapel and how it subsequently may have affected their broader experience of everyday life. This was done using a series of interviews and questionnaires.

In this study, and a follow-up carried out by Rick Doblin in 1992, nearly all participants who had received psilocybin rated the experience as highly profound, leaving a positive impact on not only their faith but also wider aspects of their life, including their personal relationships and appreciation of new experiences. Those who had not received psilocybin had far lower recall of the events of the experiment, and hardly any reported such long-term positive effects. Whilst Pahnke's study has previously been criticized for minimizing the sometimes difficult experiences of most participants whilst under the influence of psilocybin (including the use of a tranquilizer on one particularly anxious subject), it emphasizes the positive long-term psychological effects of even a single psychedelic experience.

Modern Day Studies

In the decades since the Good Friday Experiment, devoted research to the effects of psilocybin and its benefit to humanity has largely been hampered by legal issues. Up until the mid-'60s, psychedelics, including psilocybin,

More research needs to be funded into psilocybin as medicine.

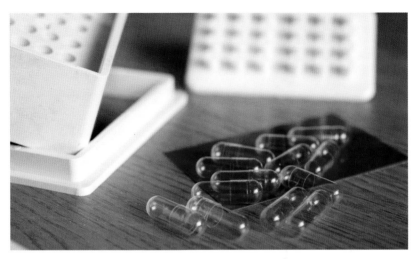

Mushroom capsules allow for easy and exact dosing.

were legal and frequently used in psychotherapy to help treat a number of conditions. However, the explosion of psychedelics into the counterculture was ultimately what led to their eventual ban by the Nixon administration in 1970 under the Controlled Substances Act.

Until very recently, conducting the most basic research required such a great deal of paperwork and bureaucracy to obtain even a miniscule amount of psilocybin that most high-quality, large-scale studies were rendered effectively unfeasible. This is not just the case with psilocybin; a researcher at the University of Sydney recently revealed that his team was paying up to $10,000 for a gram of mephedrone for laboratory research into the drug while it was selling for $30 per gram on the streets.[13] Today the tide is slowly turning, but society's long-held perception of psychedelic research as "weirdo-fringe" still holds back funding, resulting in small studies that can only generate limited conclusions. Few organizations possess the resources and dedication to the cause of applying modern scientific rigor to the initial findings of researchers of the late '50s and '60s.

Cluster Headaches

Some of the most promising research over the last decade or so has centered on a potential treatment for cluster headaches. Also known as suicide headaches, these are cripplingly painful attacks that often drive

Mycelium under the microscope. This is rhizomorphic growth.

sufferers to extreme measures; the suicide rate amongst sufferers of cluster headaches is in excess of 20 times the national average.[14] Following anecdotal evidence from one sufferer who escaped the pain of his condition by taking LSD for three years, only to have the headaches return as soon as he stopped, the scientific community has been timidly embarking on research into psilocybin and its effects on cluster headaches. In 2006, Yale School of Medicine published results of testing in which 53 cluster-headache patients used psilocybin mushrooms or LSD. Of the 26 patients who used psilocybin, 22 reported that ingestion of the mushroom aborted an attack. Even more amazingly, 52% of all subjects experienced a total cessation of their cluster period, with a further 42% experiencing partial to total cessation of their cluster period.

Forty-two percent of the subjects in this trial achieved their results at sub-hallucinogenic doses. This has led to the testing of a compound known as BOL-148, a non-psychoactive and chemically altered cousin of LSD, which produces a slight "drunk" effect but nothing more. While testing has been limited thus far, a number of sufferers have reported cessation and ongoing remission of the headaches, while others have reported remission of a month or more at a time. It should be clear to us all that this is research worth expanding and investing in.

Microdosing

You may have heard, in the last year or so, about microdosing—the "hot new business trip" that has Silicon Valley workers feeling more creative, more productive, happier and generally better equipped to deal with the stresses, strains and challenges of their lives. They've been achieving this by taking "sub-therapeutic" amounts of LSD or psilocybin mushrooms, therefore drawing on all the positive effects of hallucinogenics without experiencing a "real trip."

Of course, microdosing has been around a lot longer than this, and those hard little workers in Silicon Valley aren't the only ones to love it. People have been taking small amounts of psychedelic drugs for as long as they've been taking large amounts of it; as we mentioned earlier in this book, Terence McKenna posits the theory that psilocybin mushrooms may have helped early humans by heightening their senses and stamina, enabling them to hunt more effectively. However, it was American psychologist James Fadiman who popularized the practice amongst tech entrepreneurs and others when, at a psychedelic research conference (yes, such things exist) in 2011, he discussed survey data he had collected from microdosing experiments. This data included use of microdoses as an alternative to drugs like Adderall and as a way to alleviate conditions like depression and chronic-fatigue syndrome. The survey respondents told him that they were better creative thinkers when microdosing, more open to new ideas and increasingly able to search for innovative solutions.

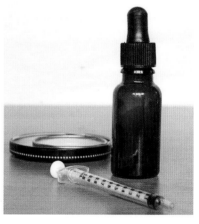

Unlike most interactions that we have with drugs, the point of microdosing is *not* to get high. The goal

Microdosing is easiest with our Basic Alcohol Extraction on page 304.

is to take an almost imperceptible amount in order to stimulate creativity, focus, stamina and a general sense of well-being without any of the swirly-reality visuals and the intense hallucinations of higher-dose psychedelic trips. With a microdose, you tap into all the most useful and useable effects of psilocybin whilst avoiding those that remove you from the world of functioning humans.

Our experiences with microdosing have echoed those reported by James Fadiman's experimenters. We have noticed that even at the smallest doses, we find ourselves looking around a lot more and appreciating the beauty of life; you notice the great lighting in your favorite café, or the awesome perspective you get on a city on your walk home from work. You're more energetic and enthusiastic, and you feel like you can tap into things in your mind more easily, recalling memories or facts and answering questions more fully and efficiently. You find yourself laughing and smiling a lot more for no real reason, and you're more likely to answer a colleague's query with "Yeah! Let's figure it out" than with "Ugh, all right I'll deal with it." There is no peak and no comedown, and no dip in well-being afterwards.

Not a bad harvest from a PF Tek jar!

It's sort of like being on a mood enhancer or an antidepressant but without any of the terrible side-effects, which is exactly how many people are using microdoses. Many people have reported that microdosing helped them deal with depression, OCD, ADD and eating and anxiety disorders, making psilocybin a potentially viable alternative to the selective serotonin re-uptake inhibitors (SSRIs) that are routinely prescribed for such conditions, and which come with the risk of suicidal thoughts, sexual dysfunction, restlessness, intercranial bleeding and, worst of all, pleasureless orgasms.

However, slight downsides can include a tendency to be distracted and be slightly overemotional, thanks to the increased sense of empathy. We experience these anyway, so we simply have to recognize this and apply ourselves to committed concentration while microdosed. We also avoid watching sad movies because that's a real bummer anyway. For reasons of personal responsibility and being a good human, don't do anything while microdosed that you wouldn't do after a beer or two.

We prefer microdosing with shrooms rather than LSD because we prefer shrooms in general (they never seem to bring up those soul-crushing, introspective self-criticisms that you (we) can sometimes get on acid), and also because the "body high" of a shroom microdose is less intense, and

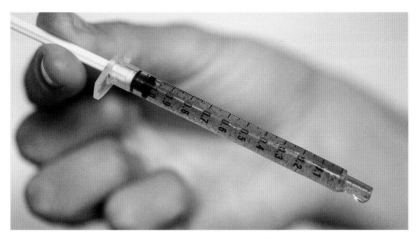

You can ensure a consistent and accurate microdose with an alcohol extraction.

therefore more manageable, than on acid. It's also a lot easier to accurately dose with a liquid psilocybin extraction than it is with a tab of acid; while it might be fine for some people to throw a tab of acid into a glass of juice and take just a sip in the morning, we like to know exactly how much we're taking at any one time.

Of course, it's entirely possible that a portion of the effects of microdosing are down to the placebo effect. Those of us who have a fair amount of shrooming experience can be induced into feeling those effects by the mere suggestion of consuming shrooms, and this might go some way to explaining why microdosing is effective. If this is the case, we think it's fantastic.

How Much Is a Microdose?

Dosing, as ever with psychedelics, is entirely subjective. It's generally accepted that a microdose is one-tenth of a "therapeutic" dose; that is, a dose that you would usually use to get the full effects. You'll read that other people take anywhere between .01 and .05 grams, but as already discussed in this book, the effect that shrooms have on you can be affected by the strain of shrooms, the extraction method, how much you've eaten, how much you've drunk, whether you've consumed any other drugs in the last 24 hours and so on and so on. What you're planning to do while microdosed may also affect your dosing choice; if you're sitting at home or in a café and writing a novel you might chance a higher dose, while if you've got to go into an office or work environment and be a highly functioning human being that's accountable to others, you may want to err on the side of caution. It's all going to be trial and error for you.

We strongly suggest starting with the lowest possible dose and working your way upwards. 0.1 of a gram is a good choice for your first microdose. If it's too little and you don't feel anything, you've lost nothing; your day has just been as it would have been anyway. If you don't get the desired effects from this, try 0.2 the next time. Continue increasing the dose by 0.1 of a gram until you notice a difference. In order to find the upper limit of microdosing (if you want to do this), we recommend setting aside a day away from other people and from any commitments or responsibilities. In the morning, take just a little more than what you've found to work. If this is too much like a real "trip," then you can just wait it out and have a great time doing whatever you want to do in the privacy of your own home, calling in reinforcements if necessary. If you find that you can still function as normal and actually get more of your desired effects, then that's fantastic. You can now dose at that level without worry. You may find that keeping a diary of your experiences on each dose is helpful, as it can be difficult to accurately compare doses on memory alone. Keep a small notebook and record how you're feeling, your productivity levels, any changes in behavior, etc., and compare your notes when you're back to base point.

Our Microdosing Method

The measurements given here are what we would consider a good starting point for most. The shrooms we used were ones that had previously produced a fairly intense trip at 0.75 grams to 1 grams, and we found that 0.1 grams produced the effect that we wanted from microdosing. As always, you can scale this up if necessary.

The extraction we used was the Basic Alcohol Extraction detailed in Chapter 13. This extraction contained 10 grams of active material in 20 ml of alcohol, meaning that 1 ml contained one 0.5 gram mushroom dose.

To create microdoses, we took 2 ml of the Basic Alcohol Extraction and added this to 100 ml of orange juice. We then split this into 10 ml portions and put each 10 ml portion into one compartment of an ice cube tray, then popped the ice cube tray into the freezer. This created

A well-dried shroom. This is now ready for storage or use.

10 separate microdoses of 0.1 grams per ice cube. We then popped each dose out and melted it into a larger glass of juice or simply waited for it to melt in a glass and took it like a shot.

You can use any liquid of your choice for this; juice was a good choice for us, as it tastes good and is relatively healthy. You can even just use water, though we'd recommend something with a strong taste to counteract the taste of the extraction itself.

One concern with this method is the breakdown of the active ingredient at room temperature. This is why we recommend freezing the psilocybin-containing OJ into dosed cubes.

Most people advocate microdosing in the morning, but this is largely because most people want to feel the effects throughout the workday. Realistically, you can microdose at any time of day, though you should avoid taking it too close to bedtime just in case you struggle getting to sleep.

James Fadiman recommends a one-day-on, two-days-off approach to regular microdosing, and this is certainly one that we can get behind. While it's always best to keep your regular drug usage as conservative as possible, we've found that this is a schedule that keeps tolerance low and still keeps the effects at a desirable level. Even one day a week isn't a bad amount of usage to try. You'll quickly decide what works best for you.

It's worth mentioning that if you're keen to try microdosing, it's good to have clearly defined expectations or goals. If you're using microdosing simply as a reason to take mushrooms on a daily basis or to escape the sharp edges of a reality that you're not entirely happy with, then you should be striving towards a change in that reality rather than finding an excuse to get away from it. We don't condone regular use of psychedelics (or anything) as a way to avoid real life.

You'll also have to consider that one day you'll have to stop. Let's say you find that microdosing works perfectly for you; it stimulates you to work better and with longer periods of creativity and concentration. Maybe you start doing it a couple of times a week and your work life is greatly enhanced. One issue here is that you can become reliant on the microdose; if you start to feel that you work best while dosing, it's incredibly difficult to convince yourself that you're still good without it. Perhaps you're in an environment where you can microdose till the day you die; that's great. Most of us aren't. Not to be Professor Buzz Killington about this, but remember, one day you'll likely have to stop microdosing and you need to be able to be a happy, productive, functioning member of society with no assistance at all. This isn't to say that you shouldn't microdose; this is just to say that you need to always be able to come back to Earth.

On a final note, don't go down the "well, more is probably better" route that we've also found ourselves on at some point in our drug-taking history. Find a microdose that works for you and stick to it, only increasing the dose if you find that your increasing tolerance renders the original dose ineffective. Getting carried away and taking more than what really constitutes a microdose will lead to you reaching what has been termed "limbo," in which you're not high enough to be tripping but you're too high to handle your everyday activities and responsibilities either. There's literally no point in being in this limbo. It's the worst of both worlds. Microdose for productive, happy days or dose higher for the real trip; don't find yourself trapped somewhere in between.

Footnotes

12. Michael Pollan. *The New Yorker*, February 2015. See online: http://www.newyorker.com/magazine/2015/02/09/trip-treatment

13. Nick Kilvert. *New Science Journalism*, January 2013. See online: http://newsciencejournalism.com/01/2013/suicide-headaches-how-the-failed-war-on-drugs-is-perpetuating-the-worst-pain-that-humans-experience/

14. Robert Wold. MAPS Bulletin Special Edition, Spring 2013. Volume 23, number 1, at 34-35. See online: http://www.maps.org/news-letters/v23n1/v23n1_p34-35.pdf

Glossary

agar - gelatinous, non nutritious substance, obtained from algae, that's used extensively in labs for a variety of cell culture and microbiology techniques.

autoclave - a pressure chamber requiring elevated temperature and pressure different to ambient air pressure. In this book we use this to mean "pressure-cooked."

baeocystin – an analog of psilocybin found in psychedelic mushrooms.

bulk substrate – any sort of nutritious material that can be colonized in large amounts.

candy thermometer – otherwise known as a sugar or meat thermometer.

canning retorts – a piece of equipment used for the sterilization of cans.

casing – a non nutritious "casing" layer on top of the substrate.

coconut coir – a material made from the fibrous inner shell of a coconut.

contamination – the unwanted presence of a contaminant or foreign body in a material.

coprophilous – something that grows or lives on dung.

double tub – a bulk substrate growing-chamber made from two tubs, one inverted on top of the other.

dunk and roll – a method used with PF Tek cakes whereby you soak them in water then roll them in dried vermiculite.

field capacity – the amount of water that remains in the soil after the excess water has drained away.

grain-to-grain – the inoculation of un-colonized grain by the introduction of colonized grain.

gypsum – a soft sulfate mineral.

hygrometers – an instrument used for measuring the moisture content in the air.

hyphal tips – the ends of long, branching fungal structures.

in vitro – outside of a living body and inside an artificial environment; in this context, inside a jar.

inoculation – the introduction of a substance, in this case a spore solution.

inoculum – the source material for inoculation, in this case a spore solution.

monotub – a dual purpose incubation and fruiting chamber for bulk substrates.

pasteurization – a process that uses high temperatures to kill off unwanted bacteria.

PDA – Potato Dextrose Agar: a micro-biological growth media made from agar and potato dextrose broth.

Penicillium – a genus of mold.

perlite – a naturally occurring volcanic glass with high water content.

PF cakes – the substrate for your PF Tek method.

PF Tek – Psylocybe Fanaticus Technique; an indoor growing-method popularized by Robert McPherson.

pinning – the process whereby mycelium move from the vegetative stage to the fruiting stage; inducing your mushrooms to begin fruiting.

psilocin – a substituted tryptamine alkaloid and a serotonergic psychedelic substance.

psilocybin – a naturally occurring psychedelic compound that appears in over 200 species of mushrooms.

psychonaut – a person that likes to trip to the moon and back.

rhizomorphic – a stringy-looking, fast-growing form of mycelial growth.

sclerotia – a hard, compact mass of fungal mycelium sometimes produced by psilocybin mushroom species.

senescence – the gradual deterioration of function of most living things; biological aging.

spawn – grain used as a substrate for mushroom growing.

spawn bag – autoclavable bags used for the incubation of grain spawn; these have a microporous filter to allow for air exchange.

spawn ratio – the amount of colonized grain used to inoculate uncolonized grain.

spores – single-celled reproductive units dropped by mushrooms to ensure propagation of the species. Each spore contains half the genetic material needed for a mature, actively fruiting mycelium.

sterilization – a process that eliminates all forms of life.

stipe – the stem that supports the cap of a mushroom.

strain isolation – the process of isolating a strain that looks particularly strong and vigorous for further cultivation and use.

substrate – the material on which a process is conducted; in this case, the material on which the mushrooms are grown.

Tek – technique.

terrarium – sealable containers that house organisms; in this case, the container for PF Tek cakes.

tomentose – a fluffy, cloud-like type of mycelial growth that grows slowly and can often be confused for contamination.

Trichoderma – a type of fungi present in all soils.

Tyndallization – fractional sterilization; a process of partial sterilization using boiling techniques.

veil – the thin membrane that covers the stalk and cap of an immature mushrooms.

vermicompost / vermicast / worm castings – the material left behind after composting via worms has occurred.

vermiculite – a hydrous phyllosilicate mineral that expands when heated.

339

Resources

There's no better resource, for anything, than the internet—though, of course, if you're doing anything that might not be considered legal in your country or state, it's a good idea to invest in something that will keep your browsing history hidden. We recommend a no-log VPN, and (of course) don't ever give your name, address or contact details to anyone you meet on forums.

During the writing of this book, and through our growing careers in general, we've been an active part of certain communities, Reddit and Shroomery being two of the main ones. There's a wealth of knowledge to be gained from the users of both these sites, and the latter can be a very serious place to gain growing knowledge. People are fallible and you should never believe everything you read online, but we've found the users of these sites to be helpful, responsive and knowledgeable.

Erowid has always been a fantastic resource for information about almost any substance you would care to put into your body and offers unbiased studies as well as a whole heap of resources. This site is fantastic for many reasons, and it's one of the few places where people can find honest information about what controlled substances will do to their bodies. For that reason (and many more), we feel it's important to donate money when possible to keep their great work going.

MAPS.org, otherwise known as the Multidisciplinary Association for Psychedelic Studies, has long been a champion of research into the uses of psychedelics. We use them as a reference regularly and fully support the great work they're doing. Again, if you have a bit of spare cash lying around, you could do worse things than to donate to this organization.

Below you'll find a fairly exhaustive list of the resources we've used and others we recommend.

Books

Cotter, Tradd. 2014. *Organic Mushroom Farming and Mycoremediation: Simple to Advanced and Experimental Techniques for Indoor and Outdoor Cultivation.* White River Junction, Vermont: Chelsea Green Publishing.

Deacon, J. W. 1980. *Introduction to Modern Mycology.* Edinburgh: Blackwell Scientific Publications.

McKenna, Terence. 1993. *Food of the Gods: The Search for the Original Tree of Knowledge: A Radical History of Plants, Drugs and Human Evolution.* New York: Bantam Books.

Nicholas, L. G., and Kerry Ogame. 2006. *Psilocybin Mushroom Handbook: Easy Indoor and Outdoor Cultivation.* Piedmont, California: Quick American, Piedmont.

Nutt, David. 2012. *Drugs Without the Hot Air: Minimising the Harms of Legal and Illegal Drugs.* Cambridge: UIT.

Oss, O. T., and O. N. Oeric. 1976. *Psilocybin: Mushroom Home Grower's Guide.* San Francisco: And/Or Press.

Russell, Stephen. 2014. *The Essential Guide to Cultivating Mushrooms: Simple and Advanced Techniques for Growing Shiitake, Oyster, Lion's Mane and Maitake Mushrooms at Home.* Massachusetts: Storey Publishing.

Stamets, Paul. 1996. *Psilocybin Mushrooms of the World: An Identification Guide*. San Francisco: Ten Speed Press.

Stamets, Paul. 2000. *Growing Gourmet and Medicinal Mushrooms, 3rd. Ed.* San Francisco: Ten Speed Press.

Stamets, Paul. 2004. *Mycelium Running: A Guide to Healing the Planet through Gardening with Gourmet and Medicinal Mushrooms*. San Francisco: Ten Speed Press.

Wayne, Rush R., PhD. 2001. *Growing Mushrooms the Easy Way: Home Mushroom Cultivation with Hydrogen Peroxide*. Online: http://www.Mycomasters.com

Websites

erowid.org

magic-mushrooms.net

maps.org

reddit.com/r/shrooms

rollitup.org

shroomery.org

thegooddrugsguide.com

TV Shows / Documentaries / Films

A New Understanding: The Science of Psilocybin. Online: http://www.anew-understanding.org.

Schultz, Mitch, Rick Strassman and Joe Rogan. 2010. *DMT: The Spirit Molecule*.

Parry, Bruce. 2005–2007. *Going Tribal* (known as *Tribe* in the UK). BBC.

Morris, Hamilton. *Hamilton's Pharmacopeia* (Vice). Online: http://www.vice.com/en_ca/series/hamiltons-pharmacopeia

Drugs Inc: Hallucinogens (National Geographic). Online: http://channel.nationalgeographic.com/drugs-inc/episodes/hallucinogens/

Index

A

M

353

About the Authors

Virginia Haze is a nomadic writer and editor with a long history of both writing about and using intoxicants in all their forms, though not always at the same time. She's written for drug culture magazines, worked on many step-by-step cultivation guides and learned to grow mushrooms under the expert tutelage of Dr. Mandrake. After beginning her growing career for personal use, she spent years perfecting her techniques and studying the science of psilocybin cultivation to allow her to grow on a commercial scale. Her specific mycological interests involve psilocybin extractions and modifying traditional grow methods. As well as sitting in her grow rooms to watch her little fungi make their way into the world, Virginia enjoys puns, '80s B-movies and making questionable life choices.

Dr. K. Mandrake is a lover of hallucinogens from both a scientific and a recreational perspective. His long and varied education has mostly centered on biology, toxicology and mycology, culminating in a PhD on the study of shrooms, which greatly influenced his home growing-methods. He cultivates all types of mushrooms (psychedelic and purely delicious) from his base in the UK, and outside of his more traditional academic position, he teaches others how to grow their own mushrooms in a sustainable, healthy and affordable way. Some say they're married to the job; Dr. Mandrake says he's married to the mushrooms. His specific mycological interests include agar work and bulk substrate methods. He enjoys turning his kitchen into a makeshift laboratory, climbing to the top of very high mountains and kicking back with a home-brewed beer to play violent videogames.

Today a young man on acid realized that all matter is merely energy condensed to a slow vibration, that we are all one consciousness experiencing itself subjectively, there is no such thing as death, life is only a dream and we are the imagination of ourselves.

Now here's Tom with the weather.

— Bill Hicks